A.I.R. Head:
Anatomy of an Artist
in Residence

by Alan Nakagawa

ISBN: 978-1-945178-97-9

Published by
Writ Large Press
a division of Writ Large Projects
Pittsburgh, PA

writlargeprojects.com

Book Design by Chynna of Monforte Studio
www.monforte.studio
Printed in USA

INTRODUCTION

In May of 2016, I left my position as a Senior Public Arts Officer for the Los Angeles Metro. I worked for the agency for twenty-four and a half years and if you add the previous two years I worked for the Social and Public Art Resource Center, it was the end of a lot of time administering public art projects in my hometown, Los Angeles.

Although I had always had a paralleling art practice, specifically with non-profit arts collective Collage Ensemble Inc. (1984-2011), I had an opportunity to focus on my solo art practice full-time. Transitioning out of the resolved 501(c)3 of Collage, the number of opportunities as a solo artist began to grow. From 2016 through 2020, I would engage with the following institutions as an artist-in-residence:

2016, Myth No Myth, Mini Artist Residency, Getty Villa
2016-17, Creative Catalyst Artist in Resident, Los Angeles Department of Transportation
2017-19, Artist in Residence, Great Streets, Office of the Mayor, City of Los Angeles
2017, Artist in Residence, Echo Park Film Center
2017, Artist in Residence, Printmaking Invitational, Cerritos College
2018, Creative Strategist Artist in Residence, Los Angeles County Library
2018-19, Little Saigon; Six Field Trips Generating, Artist in Residence, Orange County Museum of Art

2018-19, UNFINISHED PROOF NINOMIYA, Artist in Residence, Ninomiya Photography Archive, Praxis Art, California State University Dominguez Hills
2019-20, Invisible Tea House, Artist in Residence, Pasadena Buddhist Temple, Side Street Project

Contrary to popular belief, artist-in-residencies don't necessarily mean you have a place to stay at the organizations. For instance, the Los Angeles Department of Transportation doesn't have a dorm or hotel or at least not one that I know of or was ever shown. Rather and in these opportunities, they are/were experiments that added the artist's creative process into an existing infrastructure that often has never worked closely or integrally with an artist. I have heard of such practices for think tanks in Silicon Valley or the RAND Corporation. The opportunities do not have to result in an artwork but rather the possibility of intervention of a different perspective or process, in the same way you would add any professional thinker. By changing the content of the engine of a process, you change the context of the process and therefore the outcome.

I started to receive requests from artist and arts professionals, often someone I've never met, who wanted to meet with me regarding all of these opportunities. It's usually over coffee somewhere in Koreatown. They wanted to know how I got all these opportunities. I never had a clear and simple answer during these sit downs and often would leave these meetings thinking of other things I could have shared. I guess it wasn't clear in my mind. *How did all this happen?* This book is my attempt to answer this question in a comprehensive manner.

Part of it is timing, the rest is in this book.

At the start of my new solo artist trajectory, I had re-examined my artistic hopes and goals having resolved Collage Ensemble Inc.. I wanted to make art that in some ways helped people. I decided to end my decades of collaborative practice and focus on developing a body of work that spoke to my interests in sound, listening and memory.

First, I felt I needed to expand my sense of scale, so I gave myself a curriculum to go see Earthworks. I started with Lightening Field (Walter De Maria) in New Mexico. There's much written about this work but the most important impression I was left with was how the artist crafted an experience that begins far before you are actually at the site. The work begins once you commit to going and that means the moment you RSVP online. The realization of De Maria's masterful orchestration on this conceptual level blew me away.

> My friend Aandrea Stang had organized a tour of Earthworks years earlier for Smithson's retrospective when she worked at the Museum of Contemporary Art in Los Angeles. She had worked with Hikmet Loe. Hikmet is an Earthwork specialist and has written extensively on Smithson's work. When I mentioned

my self-prescribed curriculum, Aandrea introduced me to Hikmet and that was the start of an amazing friendship and education.

To date, I've visited, either by myself or with Hikmet and Aandrea: Lightening Field (Walter De Maria), Spiral Jetty (Robert Smithson), Double Negative (Michael Heizer), Sun Tunnels (Nancy Holt), Amarillo Ramp (Robert Smithson) and I would include in this grouping Noah Purifoy's Desert Art Museum in Joshua Tree and Salvation Mountain at the Salton Sea. We have plans to go see Broken Circle/Spiral Hill outside of Amsterdam at some point as we continue this fun research.

* *

Chiwan Choi (Writ Large Projects) said it was worth writing about these experiences. I've always felt that nothing I do is particularly original. My only "originality" has always been that I consistently "do." My friend and painter Celia Ko once said to me that I was an art making machine. I have mixed feelings about this analogy. I am not sure how to digest being a machine but I appreciate her candor. My life circumstances have allowed me the privilege of access to art history and practices, time and space to work, and a generous support system of community and resources.

* *

I'm not going to dwell too much on my public art

management history, although it is integral to my development as an artist and a citizen of Los Angeles. Two things. One, when I was an undergraduate student at Otis, our painting instructor Emerson Weolffer commented on my dedication to creating multi-media performances for my assignments. He said, "Oh, you're a producer. You should make films." He said it in a way that was part of his ribbing or joking personality and I think at the time I felt put down but now I realize he was right. I have always had the knack for organizing and implementation. Two, maybe this comes from being the oldest cousin and always being responsible for the little ones at family events or maybe it comes from growing up in my parent's restaurant and understanding management and logistics. The bottom line is it led me to project management of public art projects and all of the individual components it takes to process creativity for communities. It would seem that this skill and experiences came in handy when working within government, private and organizational structures within the context of art intervention.

* *

What did I learn from all those years of working in government? instigating corruption is social brutality

* *

I have had the privilege of speaking in front of audiences about my work at public events, community meetings and schools. In some shape or form, this manuscript or book is a collection of bits and pieces of what I've said at these events with the addition of the backstory. It's not just about traversing the art community as an artist. I'm also a single father, the son of immigrants and someone deeply rooted in his hometown.

* *

I'm forgetful, having a hard time remembering names or where I met someone or where did I hear a piece of music or see a certain artwork. Who was that again? What was the name of that piece? Once on KPFK FM, I heard someone talk about the power of rosemary water or tea, that it improves memory. I've been drinking it ever since. Outside these moments of forgetting, of the constant mode of trying to remember, not being able to recall, are the rare moments of clarity; remembering, sometimes. Is it like when a person with Parkinsons who all of a sudden remembers, is "back," consciousness rising to the surface of "now" and they wonder where she/he/they was, awaking from a dream but in a groggy state. "Oh hello, yes, I know/am aware/am awake/am back/for how long? from where? where am I? What happened?" Refreshed and rebooted but with the fear of returning to that state of purgatory. Oliver Sacks speaks about this in his book *Awakenings*. Remembering is awakening. This is freedom.

* *

I love writing songs and privately singing songs but I am terrible at memorizing lyrics. I don't think I could ever play live without a music stand in front of me. Consequently, I've become a sound artist who relies on recording, live improvisation, working in my home studio, and on my lap top. I make it here and then I present it over there relying on technology and equipment. This reliance on technology is an extension of my sketch pad. It's all drawing to me. I have to draw it, write it down, record it and then it's out of my head and that makes room for the next idea because remembering doesn't work for me. I need to place the idea somewhere so I feel safe I can move on to the next idea. Then I can come back to all these ideas, often connecting the dots from one to the other and often this is how I make my work. It's certainly how I made this book. It's like my external hard drive. The technology remembers for me.

* *

Perinatal/ prenatal psychology was introduced to me in High School by the school's therapist Dr. Wendy McCord. I've never experienced it but she did and hearing her talk about it really impacted me.

Dr. McCord had met a practitioner Dr. Barbara Findeisen. I think she or someone she studied with was from the original group trained in Primal Therapy. As I recall, the objective was to go back to the point of birth and prior to birth. What an amazing objective! There's something about my approach to sound and working with others that is related to this practice. I hope to someday delve more into this.

＊ ＊

Pluralism is the bull in the china shop. You break it you buy it. Who benefits from the fear of breaking the metaphoric dishware? Why didn't pluralism flourish during Modernism? Why was Post-Modernism celebrated so much while pluralism glanced over? Who benefited from that?

＊ ＊

A dream: *Let's re-avert our attention from the infinity of chronology both away from "was" and the "will be," re-avert it to the "now," dissect the narrative of the "now" into the moment, connect it to the memory, find meaning or value in "here."*

Remembering that time and slicing it into that half-second into that micro-second, nano-second and onward or inward, until we realize the slicing will never end. There will always be time to subdivide and unlike a sense of falling (like the fine line between respect and fear) find comfort in the forever of this dissection, breaking it down even further, forever or let's use the word "infinity," that there will always be something to cut in half, to fraction. It will never end; onto the next idea.

I thought about this a lot, starting in the fourth grade, when the teacher drew on the chalkboard, that horizontal line with the arrows at both ends and the zero in the center. -3, -2, -1 to the left and 1, 2, 3 to the right but what about in between? Isn't that infinity too, isn't it? This was a manifest of my ongoing balance of the material and the spiritual; the external world and the family world and/or the American and the Japanese-American. I was so happy when I discovered the movie, *The Adventurers of Buckaroo Banzai Across the 8th Dimension*. It was the first time I heard anyone else talk about this idea.

* *

poem
poem is a loaded term
too much responsibility
testimony is better
i'll use testimony

* *

Alien life = You in a parallel universe

* *

It's not just who you know but how you sustain the conditions for them to keep wanting to know you

* *

I've had this reccurring dream of thick liquid X's and O's, counting backwards, brownish fuzzy blurry sepia tinted dream, the intoxication of musk, the smell of roasted Japanese Beetles, like roasted almonds, not like the descriptive label in a bag of coffee roast but steaming from the guilt of having killed all those insects, the claustrophobia of the cocoon, where the tactility of your panicked breath becomes apparently warm, where breath chokes from all that counting; nonchalant panic that can't be verbalized.

**

Why is a cheese knife a cheese knife? I stare at it, graceful, efficient design but I have no idea why it works way better than a butter knife. We all have jobs. They are different jobs. Why do we argue and wall off others, because essentially, they don't have the same job as we do? Did you listen to that podcast about how managers tend to hire staff who are like themselves when in fact to build a stronger management team, having diverse mindsets and ways of working is the way to go? I have found that few managers have the skill to assemble a diverse team. This is due in part to social and managerial psychosis. This is what bureaucracy is. This is why most government and corporate structures are top-heavy.

**

Maybe infinity is the space between having a hunch and remembering?

**

Tip of my tongue sounds good but it was never the tongue, we use the tongue, maybe it's literal, maybe it's a metaphor or maybe because there's too much talking? (the over used tongue) Maybe if we used the tongue less, we would remember more?

**

Art Openings:
My message to the kind folks who come to see my art work; I'm sorry there's an (art) opening but we do like to celebrate. I'm sorry that's the only time you'll see my work. That's not what I hoped for when I conceived the work. That's not the intended memory. If you have the luxury to come back, with fewer people or no other people in here, maybe, ideally, when no one else is in the building, that's the time you'll have any chance of this working. It'll not work at the art opening, unless of course, you are the only one who shows up to the opening.

**

The challenges of reading aloud in front of an audience:

Sometimes read like a list, like the things you wrote down to purchase at the grocery store. Each item written at a different time, documenting the actual moment or near the moment you realized your need for it; to buy it again. Each item, representing time and need and privilege and luxury and inventory.

Why, poet or lecturer, do you recite your work in monotone, as if it were a grocery list? Like it doesn't matter? Isn't your written word sacred? You spit words like a bored child at church. You don't get a trophy for memorizing your own poem. Maybe the words should stay on the page? Or, treat the performance as a separate art form? It has history too. I know you know that. But you act like I wouldn't notice but I did.

* *

In the very few workshops I've conducted about podcasting and oral history technique, I spent time talking about microphones. I compare our hearing organs to the technology of the microphone and amplification or recording. Essentially, the translation of sound waves to electricity and then back to sound waves is keenly similar to our hearing mechanism or at least it is to me. Three dimensions into two dimensions but back out to three dimensions. One's mastery of how to use a microphone is not so different from how we might listen to a conversation during a bustling dinner party. Your focus and proximity to the person you are "listening" to and how well you engage in listening is similar to how you vocalize into a microphone, how well you are aware to the fidelity of your sound and the relationship to that sound as it's being translated by the microphone into the room you're addressing or tool you're recording onto.

Maybe we can simplify it to "awareness"? How well something is recorded, how well you comprehend what's being said, how well you amplify what you are saying is predicated to awareness. How many times have we all been in a situation where the speaker at a panel or talk decided not to use the microphone for one reason or another. She/he/

they, may be thinking they possess an orator's voice powerful enough to be heard in the room they are in? If so, why was there a need to go to the trouble of installing an amplification system? There might even have been a sound check before the audience arrived. More importantly, now the speaker has to say everything at top loudness. What if she/he/they are talking about sensitive issues or requires a dynamic range of voice volume? That's very difficult to do without training. It's especially difficult to sustain, over a period of time. Lastly, what if there are audience members (like me), who no longer have the 20 db to 20,000 db hearing I was born with (if I was born with it)? Awareness is key especially if you find yourself in the position of communicating to a group of people and in this case a room full of people. Nobody wants to be ineffective and nobody wants to listen to someone who is ineffective. If you have to yell the entire lecture, how effective could you possibly be?

**

Maybe I should start the book like this; a few notes:

Music; originality and methodology. My main instrument is the drums. I love sound and I love music and I love making sound/music. I'm constantly studying and hungry for sound and music information. I once went to a drum workshop at West LA Music by master drummer Steve Gadd. This was in the 90's. He humbly said that nothing he played was invented by him. What he saw as his craft was to thoroughly listen to the music (and he really spent time to speak to the craft of listening) and then respond to what he felt the music needed by combining a little something from this idea and inserting a little something from this other idea and in this way, using the legacy of drumming. He developed brand new combinations of existing ideas that fit the project in front of him. I would call that hybridity or maybe it's Post Modernism? I have always taken Gadd's lesson to heart. It's a mindset I had always gravitated towards. Gadd really made it clear to me what this consciousness, in the context of making art, was. Cultivate your senses and build your arsenal of tools/ strategies; listen. Listen first, the response that fits best will make itself known. I've utilized this approach in almost every art opportunity I've had.

SECTIONS:

PROGRAM

A.I.R.

access
opportunities
to dream
to acknowledge
to immerse
to respond
where freedom is defined
using creative strategies
bridging toward meaning
what is hidden?
why is it hidden?
who benefits from something being hidden?
restoration
of artifacts
of dignity
of humanity
of faith
to be welcomed into sub-culture
with fresh eyes
dignity
reverence
artists process
trained eye
connects the dots
acknowledge the dots
zoom into the dots
where dots become planes and surfaces
surfaces like land
instigating participation
conditioning the friendly

the proverbial welcome mat
deeply rooted in the land
is history
where time is malleable
where memory is meaningful
the choreography of remembering
where voice rings true
where the quiet is acknowledged
where the quieted are acknowledged
where the silenced are acknowledged
to instigate listening to perspectives
reassign narrative
to add layer
to unpeel layers
to create safe zones
to embrace the magical
to increase color, contrast and clarity
to embrace the blurry, faded and softened
to keep it simple
to vibrate truth
to give permission
to ask for permission
to accept permission
to voice gratitude
to deepen meaning
to utilize tools
to deepen practice
to honor vocation
where family is organic
where we hold hands and grow
where science is way
where religion is way
where knowledge is way

where we listen
where we don't have to speak
where we grow
where we surprise ourselves
who we are
who we become
who we were
when is now
when it is time
when you say it's time
when it's ok
when it's not ok
when I trust you
when you trust me
when you remember
when the dust settles
when we do the work

INTENTIONS AND STRATEGIES

Sound works; I am committed to the investigation of listening strategies. My sound practice is rooted in the American classic tradition and my love for audio recording and constructing. Originally, I was a painter but my love for music gradually pushed me towards inter-disciplinary forms of work because it more accurately resembled the language construct of my thoughts not to mention our experiences. Though I still paint, sound-based inter-disciplinary practice is my creative garden of choice. I'm still a portrait and landscape painter. It's just that my paint is interdisciplinary.

I often recommend to participants of my sound works to hold balloons and wear ear plugs while experiencing my noisy installations, sculptures and/ or performances. My soundscapes rely on specific placements of speakers to the body. I am not only trying to recreate or simulate the acoustics of architecture but create a *third space*; a creation of a non-existing space by combining the recordings of different spaces; mashing the acoustics of places.

I once gave a presentation in a class at California State University Northridge for artist Kim Abeles' art class. The presentation was part lecture and part sound performance. Afterwards, a student and her translator came up to me. The student appreciated what I said but she couldn't appreciate the sound portions because she was deaf. She kindly recommended that the next time I do a presentation to announce if there's anyone deaf in the audience that I would have balloons available. It took me several years to get to a point where I would utilize this strategy but a key experience that inspired the trajectory was my first experience of the *Sound Bath* at the Integratron in Joshua Tree, California. The sound bath experience is a complete immersion in pure tones, experienced in a perfect all wood dome; where the cyclical movement of tones generated by rubbing large quartz bowls tuned to the frequency chakras of the body, flow through you with no dissonance. Pure tones cyclically revolving in perfect acoustics.

The Integratron sound bath is the closest experience I have had that is like a "musician's" experience; the same sensation of sound and sound generation. As a drummer, I have always wondered about this, that is, as I play, the audience is not experiencing what I think I am generating. I get the immediacy of my musicianship, the resonance of my instrument and what I hear I am playing. The audience does not get the same projection of sound or resonance of what I am playing and vice a versa, I am not experiencing what they are experiencing.

With the Integratron sound bath, that wall dissolved. One of the objectives of my work is for the participant to feel that she/he/they are completing the resonance of the work while perhaps experiencing a sensorial practice under unique parameters and at times control those parameters.

Another advantage of using balloons and ear plugs is that it focuses or rather refocuses the body memory we have in regards to hearing. Like changing a color photograph into a black and white photograph, what is being communicated becomes sharper and more comprehensible. By doing so, a perceived simplification is exercised; concise mode. Similarly, ear plugs, are a symbol for your brain to say: "although this is sound, this is less about hearing." The balloons, held at fingertip, catch the frequencies and vibrate. The finger tips realign soundwaves as tactile rather than only auditory or more specifically redefine what auditory means. It is simulating exactly what your body is experiencing but we have been conditioned to pay less attention to this and more to what our "ears" give us. We say we hear with our ears but in fact, we hear with our bodies that includes our ears. In addition, we hear with our brains but perhaps that gets too complicated for this essay because, then, we get into memory and projection.

I like going to contemporary dance performances in theaters, squint, and watch the moving bodies become one with the stage light projection. I believe I was in college when I first experienced this. I may have gotten bored or something and as my eyes started closing, I saw the beam of light on the stage merge into the dancer's body. At the time, I was also studying artist Rachel Rosenthal's Do-By-Doing technique which introduced the concept of soft focus. Although a tool for a kind of meditation, it is also a tool to begin to rethink what the apparatus of senses are, especially as it relates to experiencing art and in this case, body movement on a lit stage.

As I mentioned earlier, from an early age, I was trained in the visual arts (age 9) and drumming (age 13). These are the most comfortable means for communication and self-expression for me. I practice music every day. Therefore, only words as a means to express myself and communicate and resolve concepts are not enough for me. I haven't mastered words. The world is not a place where we only speak and write. There are visual arts, music, sports, dance, etc. Only words would be like an athlete only working out by doing jumping jacks, no running, weights, etc. I read somewhere that Einstein visualized his formulas before he built the calculations. I also read somewhere that some who are blind visualize space using systems such as echo-location. They can picture the environment in their mind's eye.

Often, when talking about the conflicts and challenges of life, the beauty in life, certainly relationships, you hear the phrase, "it's complicated." That's where I like to be. That's where my art thrives. Art that is not complicated doesn't interest me much; obvious and boring when it speaks to the "surface" of life but if something is complicated, difficult to put into "words," this is where most artists like to be, on the frontlines of issues, conflicts, theories and analysis. Perhaps "complicated" is subjective. I hope my point is clear. It's complicated.

In my sound work, Peace Resonance; Hiroshima/ Wendover, I am combining the three-point interior acoustic recordings of the Hiroshima Dome and the Wendover Hangar. It is important for me to tell the participants the histories of these places before they engage with the sound piece. This piece could work without the participants knowing about the history of these historic spaces but it wouldn't have the weight. By mashing these two spaces, talking about the journey of producing the piece and the fact that I am Japanese-American and that my family is from Hiroshima, forms and informs the work, in part, as a self-portrait. It's a landscape painting too. It's complicated.

THE WANDERING MIND

Patchouli is a very specific scent. No one I grew up with wore patchouli. I equate it with alternative medicine, spiritualists and homeopathic herbs. When I first smelled that oil, it was in the fourth grade. (I wouldn't learn what its name was till I was a young adult working near Venice Beach.) That day, we had a substitute teacher. I'd seen her before. She often monitored the playground. She was petite, physically fit, had a button nose, wore alternative cotton bell bottoms and her eyes had eyeliner that evoked Cleopatra. After our lunch, we were back in the classroom and it was a hot L.A. afternoon outside so she must have sensed a general fatigue and maybe restlessness.

She stood at the front of the classroom and asked, "Do you want to learn how to meditate?" I didn't even know what that was and my guess is most of my classmates didn't either but when you're very young and you're asked by someone you think is pretty cool that sort of question, you are all in.

She said, "Let's lower all the window blinds." Some of the students carried out that task. She went and closed the two classroom doors, which evoked a kind of secret society atmosphere. She turned the light off and told us to put our heads on the desk. What she walked us through I would later learn was a simple form of Transcendental Meditation. I think we were into it. I was and actually had a focus vision that I would return to almost weekly for years.

Along the way, I picked up bits and pieces of meditation, acupressure, yoga and stretching exercises through friends, workshops, doctors and courses. Every morning, for decades, I have gone through a routine borrowing from all of these various sources; an ever-changing process that helps center me each day. Sometimes it's a quick ten-minute routine and other times it could last for a half hour.

The wandering mind is a term I learned when speaking to someone who was a practitioner of meditation. I read the book *Zen Mind, Beginners Mind* by Shunryu Suzuki. He said it's alright to wander as long as you find your way back to the centering of meditation. When I practice my creative muscle, I accomplish the most when I am somewhere in between focus and wandering, effortless journey utilizing both states of mind. Sometimes, if not all the time, this is where I come up with my most successful ideas. It's always as if it wasn't my idea at all. I feel like I'm just a vehicle for the idea. Sometimes it seems to me like the idea is obvious and it was just a matter of time that *someone* would have thought of it and carried it out. In part, I think it's my morning routine that has allowed me to be open to these moments of connection, the "Aha!" moments. When something places it in my head and then it's my responsibility to make it happen. Actually, the process to make it happen is often fueled by this external guide as well.

The wandering mind can sometimes be the *wondering* mind. It's more than a tangent. It often feels like connecting the dots is an exercise that is in fact the route of the creative process and the means to the end of art.

In recent years, I participated in ArtPlace as a panelist. Part of our job was to visit the sites of the commission finalists with the director of the program. One of the sites I got to visit was a Native American community in Martha's Vineyard. We were there only 90 minutes, much of which was a walking tour with a large group of project participants. The "community" seemed to be composed of the Native Americans and non-Native Americans who were all drawn to Native American culture. After the tour, we sat outside a historic home to talk about the process. They sat the ArtPlace Program Director and I at the head. He and I had sunglasses on. What I noticed was the Non-Native Americans sat around us while the Native-Americans ended up sitting towards the back of the group. Some of them didn't get to sit down because there were no more chairs. As the short meeting ended, it dawned on me that by wearing sun glasses, no one could see my eyes. That and the seating arrangement made me conscious of the messaging sunglasses play in the power dynamics of a meeting such as the one I'm describing here. I no longer wear sunglasses. I don't own sunglasses anymore. I got rid of them. I favor hats with visors or rims.

How you read situations and clues in a group setting or within the context of a meeting is contingent on your mental state. What are the tools to keep our awareness and perception literacy sharp? The opportunities to engage are constant. Are we ready for these opportunities?

ARTPLACE 2017

In 2017, I had the privilege of being on the selection panel for ArtPlace, a national funding source/ten-year experiment to bring major funding and resources to communities who want to make a difference by improving the quality of life through art and infrastructure. This included, throughout the year, several phone meetings, emails, site visits, two symposiums and finally the selection panel's final session which took place at ArtPlace's headquarters in Brooklyn NY. Afterward the three-day selection process ended, I wrote this to our primary contact, Javier Torres, who was amazing to work with. ArtPlace was a ten-year multi-stakeholder funding program that promoted the arts as a key component in the community planning and development process.

The multi-phase selection panel I was a part of led to the final three-day selection process where I got to meet my fellow panelist in person. We deliberated over which proposals would become the final group of projects to be awarded. The panel consisted of artists and art organizers from around the USA who were innovators in their community and gave me a grand sense of pride and a good dose of imposter syndrome. The discussions and insights they shared in this confidential forum was extremely educational and intoxicating.

Dear Javier (ArtPlace),

I knew I would really need to think about the Art-Place experience for a few days before I could gather my impressions and reply. Forgive its lateness.

I've tried hard to understand the totality of what it was we accomplished. There's probably much I don't comprehend yet. The current of the process and the flood of thoughts, perspectives and wisdom during the session from that amazing brain trust of individuals was intoxicating.

I kept finding myself between being in the moment and stepping outside the moment and marveling at our dynamic.

So, I started to write this, two days after the end of our session, while walking through the Transit Museum (Brooklyn, N.Y.), close to your office. (I got in free because I had my L.A. Metro Retiree ID with me).

I'm sitting in a historic car, one of many lined up on both sides of a retired subway platform. It's a BMT D-Type Triplex Car from 1927 that was run on the A, B, C.

Cast iron construction, dark green interior, brick red painted floor and a kind of rattan cushioned upholstery seating, has aged but is well kept.

When I enter this and really any of these trains (in this museum), the thought that reoccurs is within this historic majesty, what would have been my social status during the heyday of this train? Would I have been allowed to sit in here? To even ride this train?

I think of Isamu Noguchi who would have been a child around this time. What was it like being a child of a single white mother in Chicago around this same time? Half Japanese, the great divide was probably an intense experience for him and yet as an adult, as a professional, he found himself in the company of great minds like Buckminster Fuller and Frank Lloyd Wright and so many more.

What was his trajectory to get there? Who was his ArtPlace?

That brain trust, the panel, is an amazing machine, a ritual, a Sanctuary, and a university.

I am so grateful for your architecture.

Thank you so much for inviting me onto this (ArtPlace) Council. It was a humbling and inspiring experience.

BANDMATES

One of the things I love about my kids is that they are still friends with people they went to school with. They're currently in their mid 20's and get together on occasion to catch up with these friends, who they've known since they were little kids. In fact, both of their dearest and oldest friends are someone they have known since they were all in diapers. I'm envious of this.

The nature of my upbringing and the events that led to the death of my best friends is something that is deeply implanted in me and is somewhat responsible for the drive I seem to have. To this day, whenever I am about to participate in an event or milestone in my art career, I actually sort of speak to them, in my mind.

We'll start with Lorenzo.

Lorenzo was a brain, studied Latin and was an extremely talented pianist. We met in high school.

My parents enrolled me in Daniel Murphy, an all-male Catholic High School near Hollywood. They told me that there was a music program there so I agreed to go. When I got there, it turned out there was no music department. I was duped. So, I gravitated towards this circle of musicians in my class and that year, it just so happened, that there was Father Joseph O'Brien, the new vice principal, who championed us and got us permission to not only practice in the chapel every week but also play for the Friday Mass. He was a music major in college.

This is where I started calling myself a pagan. As the only non-Catholic in the band, I was proud to be the pagan. Every Lent, I would flaunt my meat burrito for lunch, for instance. It was a very fun and nurturing environment and I had an incredible time at this school.

Lorenzo's family was Italian, from Naples, I believe. Sometimes, we would practice at his place on Saturdays or during the summer weekdays, while his folks were at work. Lorenzo's family was very Catholic. Towards the end of practice, the phone would ring and it would be Lorenzo's Mom and we would be invited to stay for dinner. That was the thing; dinner at the Lorenzo's. They grew grapes in the back and had a small shelter where they made wine. They still had a lot of family back in Italy so they would always get these special ingredients in the mail. This is where I learned about Al Dente. This is where I learned about true Italian tomato sauce; it shouldn't suffocate the pasta but should add flavor to the flavor of the pasta; balance. This is where I learned about Italian escargot. It was always a feast and I and the other bandmates enjoyed it so much.

Lorenzo and I loved music that was a little more underground than what the other bandmates listened to. We spent a lot of time together listening to music and talking about it. There was a band called Emerson, Lake and Palmer that we adored. Lorenzo turned me onto Brian Eno, King Crimson and rare recordings by Allistor Crowley. There was one album that he was into that was sounds of exorcisms that I shied away from. He was into it. At school, while most used backpacks for their books, he would use a brief case. Lorenzo was always proper and we looked forward to a future of continuing our musical collaborations but when we were well into our senior year, things started to shift and it was decided that this band we were all in, like high school itself, would end. Oddly, I wasn't sad about it because I was already hyped up for college. Looking back on it, I wished I could have been a little bit more aware of its implications.

Lorenzo announced he was giving up music and was going to Med school at UCLA. We had never heard him talk about becoming a doctor and it was sort of out of the blue but he was a brain so it did make sense at the time.

Lorenzo went to UCLA and I to Otis Art Institute. We lost touch at first, as we both immersed ourselves into our new environments. One day, in our second year of college, I was home and I heard a noise at the front door and went to take a look. I saw Lorenzo driving away in his Volvo. There was a letter in the mailbox. It was around Thanksgiving and the letter was a thank you note for being a good friend. That was a little odd but I missed him too and later phoned him but couldn't get a hold of him. About a month later, one of the other former bandmates called to tell me that Lorenzo hung himself. The story is that he had created some elaborate system in his bedroom out of white bed sheets. When his parents and brother came home, he was hanging there, lifeless. There was some confusion that he may have been doing some sort of experiment that went terribly wrong. He was into magician culture through the local magic society. Later it was confirmed that he had committed suicide.

We were all in shock, needless to say. The funeral was intense. I remember staying after the end of the mass. I guess I was dazed. I remember just sitting there after everyone had left to go outside. It was a large crowd of people who had come to pay their respects and I just broke down and started crying. One of our former bandmates Mom, Mrs. Mitchell was very sweet and comforted me but I just lost it.

About a month later, we received unbelievable news. Lorenzo's little brother shot the father in the head and would be tried for murder. The story is that the Mom and Dad got into a fight and the Dad started beating on her. The family had firearms in the house so the little brother took out a hand gun and aimed it at his Father. It would later come out that this was not the first time they fought and the Father would get violent. It was also told to us later that Lorenzo never really wanted to become a Doctor and his grades were not promising at UCLA. We also learned, and this is so odd, he wrote an article against suicide in the school paper a half year before he killed himself.

Lastly, a year after we graduated from High School, one of our teachers died of AIDS. The morale at the high school was understandably very low and so Lorenzo brought the band together again to play for the school in memory of this teacher. In hindsight, we all believe that Lorenzo had planned his suicide at least a year before he carried it out. Getting the band together one last time was part of his bucket list.

Another friend was Lennie.

Lennie Birenbaum had a stage name, Lennie Browning. He was on TV a lot. We both went to Founders School, an experimental school; kindergarten to the ninth grade with a student body of five hundred. Our class had nine students in it and we were together for 7th, 8th and 9th grade.

Founders Church is a Religious Science organization and is still located on 6th Street near Vermont Avenue. The experimental school, however, was located in Hollywood. They rented the classroom section of the Hollywood Temple, a Jewish organization. We shared their classrooms.

Our class had four teachers. That's four teachers to nine students. So, it's no surprise that the year I graduated, the school went bankrupt and closed. We were the last graduating class of Founders School.

Founders School is where I became a drummer and

Lennie was the first musician I ever met and worked with and he was my best friend. Lennie had taken piano lessons. We wanted to really get into it so we practiced a lot. I would bring my drums over to his place. We spent so much time together. We were brothers. I called his mom, Mom. We were inseparable. Two nerds who loved music. He was really into Billy Joel, who was very popular at the time. I was into Parliament Funkadelic and the Beatles. We played so much music with no supervision so we would play for hours whereever we could.

I remember he was the first person I ever told that I loved. That's not the sort of thing my family ever said so it was part of the overall transformation that was happening to me in Middle School. Lennie introduced me to weed. I never became a user but we did have fun smoking it a couple of times and then we would make a 7-11 run and buy a bunch of snacks. I got really into Pringles and Nachos Doritos. That was my thing. I wonder what Lennie would of thought of the recent legalization of pot (January 1, 2018)?

Founders School was a trip. One teacher was Mr. James, a recent graduate of Arizona State University. He majored in psychology. A tall, thin and curly haired white dude, Mr. James was kind, intuitive and intelligent. As I mentioned, the school was experimental and we were the guinea pigs. The class was indicative of the policy of the school. There were sons and daughters from well to do families, from the inner-city, lower income communities and the middle class. Not everyone was a member of Founders School. I wasn't. Actually, very little "religion" was taught to us at the school. Every Friday afternoon, Mr. James would have us sit in a circle and we would practice We-orientation; a form of addressing the pros and cons of the week as a collective. It was very new to me and helped or at least attempted to build commonality amongst us.

Another teacher was Mrs. Von Hamver. I am not sure that's how you spell it but she was the oldest teacher. She was from Austria and was Hungarian-Jewish. She would constantly tell us we were less educated than those in Europe, which was incredible to us because at Founders School, we studied constantly. Mrs. Von Hamver would periodically tell us her experience with the Nazi's in WWII. She witnessed most of her family getting shot dead by the Nazi's and her husband was experimented on by their scientists. At that time (1976-79), he still had to get an annual blood transfusion and sometimes surgery. To us, kids growing up in Hollywood, it was very hard to relate to those images. She was a very vivid story teller and those images are still etched in my mind.

Finally, Dr. Esmeralda Fucci. Dr. Fucci was from a military family in Argentina. She told us stories about carrying around a pistol in a holster from a very young age. She was very strict and was especially demanding. She actually made a few of my class mates cry on more than one occasion. She was the most notorious instructor in our school. Once,

Dr. Fucci passed out these little red books. We were told to keep them in our desks and that we were going to study them later that week. The next day, she apologized but she would need those books back as it had been determined by the school administration that these books were inappropriate for our age level. So, we gave them back to her. It was a book on Marxism. I love this story. Till this day, I have no idea who told on Dr. Fucci about the books.

We did get to study a wide range of other books; Greek mythology, Henri Rousseau, Shakespeare and Machiavelli.

At the time, reading a Shakespeare play a week and being tested on it seemed ridiculous but now it seems like an amazing adventurer. I remember Dr. Fucci fondly. She and I got along fairly well. I gravitated towards the diverse subject matter of her classes and how she was able to relate the tropes and tribulations in these writings with what was going on in current events. It made everything we read seem real.

Once we graduated, we all went to different High Schools. Lennie went to Farifax High School, I believe. One day, he came over to show me a motorcycle he bought. I hadn't seen him in months. The motorcycle was closer to a motocross style bike but he said it was street legal. It was great to see him. We talked about getting together to play music again but a couple months after, on a Sunday morning, my brother came into my room and said that he was watching the news and they said Lennie's name, something about an accident. I called Mom and she said, "Oh honey, Lennie died this morning. He got hit by a car." I was speechless. We hung up the phone. I remember very little about the funeral. I was in a daze for months. I learned a little later that Lennie was on his motorcycle going west on 3rd Street. Down a cross street, a police car was chasing a bank robbery suspect. Unfortunately, the police car did not have their siren on. The car chase crossed 3rd Street and hit Lennie and his friend on the motorcycle. Allegedly, their bodies flew several stories into the air and the intersection was drenched in blood. They closed the street down and brought in water tanks to wash the blood away. I don't really remember anything about Lennie's funeral.

Lastly, my dear friend Todd.

Todd was the other band member in High School I spent the most time with. He played sax and I was the drummer and played acoustic guitar. We played in the school band but also played as a duet. We spent a lot of time together.

Todd's parents were divorced. We would often be at his house where his mom and sister lived but once, I got to go to his dad's apartment on Vine Street. Todd's dad was a professional actor and did a lot of voiceover work. He had a home recording studio and invited us once to record our music. Even though our band would break up after High School, Todd and I continued playing together and eventually were in a band called DADA-flex with the amazing guitarist Michael Whitmore. Unfortunately, I got immersed into my studies at Otis and with a part time job, I had too much on my plate. I needed to make a decision, so I left the group. DADA-flex went on to do really good work. As the years progressed, I completely lost touch with Todd but later learned he had become a member of a group of artists in Downtown LA, what would later become the Arts District. He had co-founded a small group of artists who started a space called Five-Bucks. Unfortunately, Todd got into heroin and heroin won.

A decade later, I saw him panhandling in Downtown LA. At the time, I was very confused with this reunion on Traction Avenue. On one hand, it was great to see him but on the other hand I didn't understand why he was trying to sell me his hat? We spoke for a bit but I realized later that I don't think he remembered who I was. The manner in which our conversation went, was very general and his answers kept going back to this hat he wanted to sell me. I did give him some cash and my business card but I never heard back from him. Years later, at a high school reunion, I learned that during his second time in prison, he was killed but no details were available.

Back in high school, Todd and I were pranksters. He had these crazy ideas. I still have a short story he wrote based on his family. Both his parents were actors so he had an amazing gift for theatrics. He lived off of Beechwood in the Hollywood Hills. I remember we would always pass by Ray Manzarek's (of the Doors) house, or one of them and that was a big deal to him. Once we were just walking around Beechwood Canyon, playing music. We found a place where we could hear an echo from the other hillside, so we kept playing there. At one point, the actor Ned Beatty (*Deliverance*) comes out in a bathrobe and says, "say fellas, I appreciate the music but Sundays are my only day off and I'm trying to sleep in, do you mind playing somewhere else?" Only in Hollywood.

There was this other time, at a music store on Santa Monica Blvd., we thought it would be funny, although, today I don't see the humor in it, if we pretended to bump into each other in the music store, having not seen each other for a while. That was the idea. It was a kind of improvisational theatre exercise. What transpired was two kids over-acting in a public space. Todd's story was that he had been in NY working as a professional saxophone player. The story he weaved was so real and funny. He was a character.

As I'm writing all this down, it's been almost four decades since I've seen these guys but once in a while, I wonder what it would have been like if they were still alive? Would we be making art together? Sometimes I'll see someone walking past me who could be an adult version of them. Would they have a family too? Would we still be friends?

CIVIL ROOTS   SERVANT

December 31, 2017, 4:01 AM

Every successful civil servant comes from a community and has great mentors. For me, it starts with my family. My mom and aunts played classical Japanese music. Some of my earliest childhood memories are sitting in the waiting area of the koto and samisen school, waiting for my aunts to finish their lesson. I think this was somewhere near the LA Produce District or maybe Boyle Heights. I think it was a house but the memories aren't clear. There was a couch and some dining chairs in a small room. Coming from down the hall was the sound of the instruments. They would start and then stop. You could vaguely hear the teacher instructing, in Japanese, and then the music would play again and then stop and more talking. This is how the hour went by. There might have been magazines, not unlike a waiting room at a doctor's office. I don't remember how I occupied myself for an hour. I must have been around six or seven.

Once a year, there would be a big festival at Elysian Park and they would play on the big stage. I liked watching the performers, the emcees and the speeches. The park was packed with other Japanese families on their picnic blankets, eating and talking. These festivals were very joyous and colorful and helped define our immigrant community.

The house I grew up in was a triplex my grandparents purchased so that the entire family could live together. My grandparents, one uncle and two aunts lived upstairs. Downstairs were two smaller units. One was for my parents, brother and I. The third unit was for my uncle, the oldest of my Mom's siblings. His name was Tomiyuki but we called him Uncle Tom. He had been in the US Army and was a musician for them stationed in Europe. Paralleling my memories of my Mom and Aunt's Japanese music was Uncle Tom's passion for classical music, jazz and big band. He studied at Los Angeles City College's music department. This would have been in the 60's, when a lot of famous jazz musicians were there. In Uncle Tom's apartment was a number of open cases with reed and brass instruments. He had a spinet piano and would often be playing records. I remember hearing classical music and John Phillip Souza at great volumes. Once, I did see him play professionally. There was a famous Japanese singer who came into town and Uncle Tom was hired to be in the orchestra. We went to go see him play. It was awesome to see him in that matching suit on the band stand. They sounded great. It was a professional gig.

Later in High School, we would go together to the Hollywood Bowl for the Playboy Jazz Festival. We got to see Miles Davis, Herbie Hancock and Chick Corea, the Toshiko Akiyoshi/ Lew Tabakin Big Band, Weather Report with Jaco Pastorius, Lionel Hampton, Return to Forever, Carmen McCrae and Sara Vaughn, just to name a few. I once went with

Uncle Tom to Marla's Memory Lane to see some live Jazz. That was the last time we went to go see a show together. He told me he stopped playing music once he got married. he got a job at a bank and raised my two cousins. I really enjoyed going to go see music with him.

Shizue Yamashiro was my first art teacher. She taught me how to paint from about the time I was in the fourth grade to the first or second year of high school. On Saturdays, we would walk upstairs into her second-floor apartment. Her living room was her studio and there would already be a still life she composed on the center table. You would sit down somewhere on this L shaped table set up in front of the still life, take out your supplies and start. First it was oil pastels, then charcoals, then conte crayons, then watercolors and then, after several years, she taught me how to paint with oil colors.

Half of the room was this area for these classes and the other half was her oil painting studio. The room got east light and was on the second floor, so the window view had trees and roof tops. The classes were one hour which was just enough time to finish one drawing. Sometimes you would finish early and she would say something like, "Ok, draw from your imagination." So, from early on, there was this training that differentiated between representational and imaginative imagery.

I didn't have any friends who were also into the visual arts so this weekly ritual (1973-1982) of art class wasn't something I shared with anyone. Most of my friends were musicians. So, visual art making was fairly solitary until my final year of high school.

I went to a Catholic High School, that no longer exists, called Daniel Murphy High School and for the senior year, we waved goodbye to the Dominican Order that had been in charge for decades and said hello to the Sisters of Carondolet.

The Sisters were also in charge of Mount Saint Mary's College in Brentwood and the Doheny campus near USC. In this order was Sister Francis Xavier or as we addressed her, Sister Shimotsuma. Sister was an artist, a printmaker and she began to teach an art class at our school that was incredible. It was a college-level class and her entire studio was in the room below the chapel. It was only a year but we really learned a lot in that class and between her and the years with Shizue Yamashiro, I was able to make it into Otis.

Sister shared incredible stories about growing up in Japan during World War II. There's one story that was vivid. Air raids were common and most roads in the country had these safety ditches along them. One day, the sirens went off and she and her classmates happened to be coming home from school. They all jumped into the ditches, all these students, her friends. The planes attacked. When it was over, most of them were dead. She said she lost a lot of friends that afternoon.

At Otis Parson School of Design, we got to witness this amazing faculty that represented the transition between those who came from the historic Chouinard School and those who had recently graduated from CalArts; a generational divide. On one side were folks like Emerson Woelfer, Robin Vaccarino, Helen Watson and Sam Clayberg. On the other side were folks like Carl Stone, Arlene Raven, Mike Kelly, Stephen Prina, Christopher Williams, Lita Albuquerque and Jill Geigerich. It was an intellectual blood bath. It was confusing and very exciting for us to witness.

One day, one of my professors, art critic Joan Hugo, asked if I would want to be on a performance committee. I said sure and she handed me this small torn piece of paper with an address written on it. This would have been around 1984. Joan said to show up there Monday at 5PM. That was it. There was no other detail she shared with me. I was young and naive so it never occurred to me to ask her what a performance committee was and what was the location? Where was she sending me? I just did it because Joan Hugo told me to do it.

Monday rolled around and after classes I drove to the address. It was a gray, four or five story building way in this fairly desolate part of Downtown LA. On the side of the building in bold letters were the words "WOMAN'S BUILDING." Still, I had no clue what was going on. I walked in and said I was here for the performance committee and was directed to go to the back room. There I met Liebe Gray,

Joyce Wexler Ballard, Rachel Rosenthal, Nancy Buchanan, Cheri Gaulke, Sue Maberry, Terry Wolverton and so many others. For two years, I got to be part of this amazing organization. They were so welcoming to me. I got to work with Faith Ringold, Anna Homler, Suzanne Lacy, Beverly O'Neil, Linda Nishio to name a few. It was an honor to work with so many powerful artists and be embraced by this community.

Another fluke that happened at Otis was one day, the Fine Arts Chair, Scott Greiger, pulled me aside and said they were giving me a scholarship to go to a special Saturday class. Again, just an address and time. I drove to Venice and walked into this old looking building and was told to go upstairs. In this room were other students from other college art programs and together we were taught about consensus building and community design strategies. The instructor was Judy Baca, the place was the Social and Public Resource Center and the once a week course was called the Mural Training Program. This would have been around 1985-86. It was the start of a lifelong mentorship with Judy because later in the UC Irvine MFA program, I was her Teachers Assistant. After my post grad I worked for her as the Project Coordinator for the Neighborhood Pride Mural Program for two years; and when I started as a manager for the Metro Art program, Judy's project for the Baldwin Park Metrolink Station was one of my first projects to coordinate.

At UC Irvine, where I went for Graduate school,

one of my instructors was Linda Vallejo and one day she told me about this art program she was part of and thought I should consider it. The program was called ArtsReach and was housed in the UCLA Continuing Education offices. They hired artists to teach in the prisons throughout Southern California as a form of inmate rehabilitation. For a year and a half, I taught drawing classes at the California Rehabilitation Center for Men in Norco and the California Institute for Women in Chino. It was a life changing experience. I felt I learned as much if not more than my students learned from me. Who was being rehabilitated? It would turn out to be the first and last time I ever taught an art class but it was incredible.

These experiences were invaluable training for me. I was being conditioned to empower communities by using art making as a primary tool. They made me ready for the responsibilities of running the non-profit arts collective Collage Ensemble Inc. for twenty-seven years and working as a public art project manager for Metro for twenty-four and a half years. I was conditioned and empowered to become a civil servant.

Of course, this is just a snapshot of some of my mentors and opportunities but it all led to becoming the first Creative Catalyst Artist in Residence for the Los Angeles Department of Transportation in 2016. The multi-disciplinary training I was given gave me tools I utilized during my 14 months with LADOT, which was basically the start of my solo art career.

Even though the department had never had an artist in residence, the staff I worked with could not have been more supportive. I've had the opportunity to lecture about this experience all over the US now and I have often joked by saying that during this A.I.R., no one ever said no to me. That is to say that every art idea I came up with was given the green light, was fully supported by the staff. That staff was so amazing and seasoned but I suppose I also never proposed anything that couldn't be supported. I'm still digesting what the dynamic was. I was certainly empowered to do what I needed to do and that empowerment came from the top down, so to speak, by the full directive of the General Managers: Seleta Reynolds, LADOT and Danielle Brazell, Department of Cultural Affairs. The other key to this experience was where LADOT happened to be at the time; a transitional culture shift between a car-orientation to a people mobility-orientation engineering focus. That was a great gig where I utilized everything I was trained to do and led to subsequent A.I.R. opportunities.

CONICAL SOUND:SIMON RODIA AND ANTONI GAUDI

The objective of "Conical Sound, Simon Rodia and Antoni Gaudi" was to combine dynamic field recordings of the interiors of the Sagrada Familia in Barcelona, Spain and Watts Towers in Los Angeles, into a multi-speaker installation. Conceptually, I wanted to bring Antoni Gaudi and Simon Rodia into the same aural space and in a sense have them meet each other. I wanted to play with the idea of omnipresence; hearing multiple places, being in multiple spaces and times at once, hearing multi-vantage points in the same place and time and how interiors using conical shapes may have similar acoustics; a mash up.

The Watts Towers have withstood the test of time, as was acclaimed by Buckminster Fuller in his interview on the DVD, "I Build the Towers" by Edward Landler and Brad Byer. Simon Rodia completed it in 1954 and gave it to his neighbor, in a sense, handing it to the community. The tallest tower stands thirty meters and the walls surrounding the triangular concrete base is illustrated with Rodia's signatures including imprints of his tools, his initials, broken kitchenware, discarded bottles and mosaic tile.

I received permission to conduct this recording by

Rosie Lee Hooks, Director of the Watts Towers Art Center. What resulted from my Watts Towers field recordings was a colorful sound portrait of the neighborhood as it bounced around the six-foot walls and enormous verticals during the recording. In the recording are wind, the conservationists who were working on the Towers, a train, a plane, booming bass from a car stereo and even an ice cream vendor.

I used three recorders, each on a tripod, set them up in the interior corners of Watts Towers (the foundation is triangular) and recorded seventeen minutes of audio. I set each recorder against the interior wall with the microphones facing the wall. I was shooting for bounce rather than direct sound. The end result is a dynamic three-dimensional audio documentation of a space and a time. My objective was to have an audio work that was about ambience, acoustics and the tonal personality of the space, while also documenting a moment in that spaces time.

The second recording session took place in Spain. With the support of a group of professors and graduate students from the University of Barcelona's Sound Arts Master's Program and a grant from the Department of Cultural Affairs, City of Los Angeles, I was able to execute a recording session inside the Sagrada Familia, Antoni Gaudi's masterwork.

On the day of that recording, we met in front of the construction entrance of the Sagrada. The equipment was substantial, three tripods, three recorders, video equipment and additional audio gear. We would get one night to record three-point field recordings at thirty meters, fifteen meters and finally the floor, in an empty Sagrada Familia.

With safety hats on, we took an elevator and then construction stairways to the thirty-meter level. There's a narrow walkway that wraps around the entire Cathedral and we set up our recorders at three strategic points. There were plastic sheets, air compressors, tools, cables, pipes and various stands everywhere. Although construction started in 1882, the Sagrada was still in progress and scheduled to be completed in 2028. My main contact with the University, Professor Lluis Inacenta, had arranged with the Sagrada Familia staff to lend us walkie-talkies, which made a tremendous difference in carrying out our project. We were able to communicate with ease between the three sets of teams stationed at the perimeters of the Cathedral.

Recording at thirty meters for 17 minutes allowed us to really observe the "now." You could really see and almost touch the ceiling, although it was dark. The ceiling wasn't flat. It was like an upside-down skateboard-park. You can practically see the sound move through the space.

The session at fifteen-meters was a very different experience. This is where the choir sits so it's well-lit and very beautiful. This session went easily. Seventeen minutes in silence in a space of this magnitude is meditative. The mind wanders just like the sound.

The drones, an accumulation of street noise, wind and building movement made a soundtrack of subtle noises and colors, the reverberating evidence of the cavernous interior.

Finally, we made it to the floor. By now, there was a sense of confidence, continued awe and a bit of fatigue. I think the anticipation and nervousness of the project dehydrated some of us. No food or drinks were allowed in the church and we spent over five hours recording. On the floor, the immediacy to the street is very apparent. The sound is dynamic and wild. At the floor, we could walk around with ease and there was so much more to see.

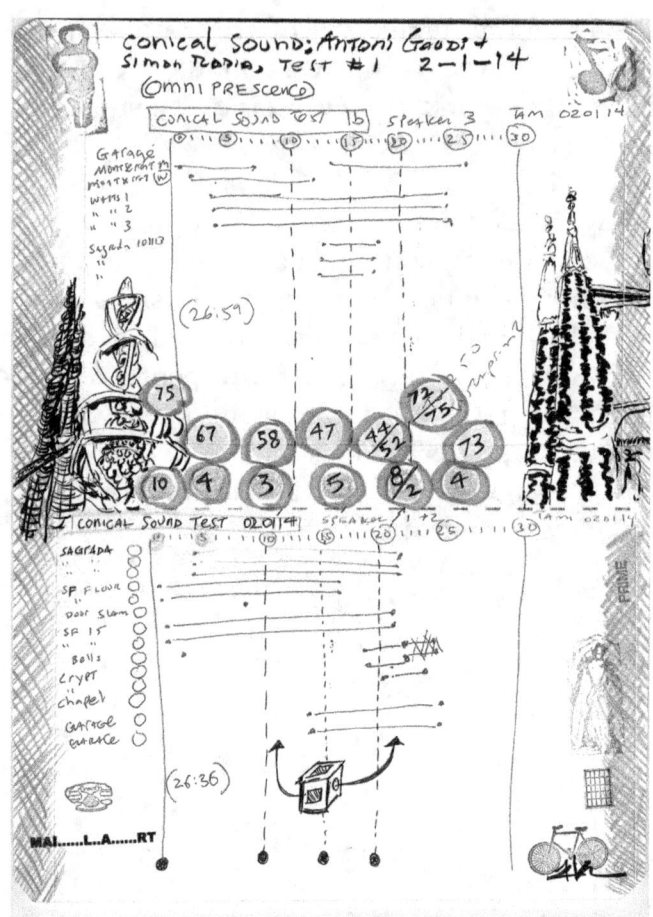

Conical Sound Test Sound Map/Reverb/Torrance Art Museum, 2014

Comparatively, the Watts Towers dynamic recording was direct and informal. The neighborhood was so alive the day of the recording that those sounds reverberated against the concrete walls and you get a warm sense of the environment the Towers sit in. The Sagrada recordings have a sense of space and at times "outer-space" as sounds from outside and those generated from the wind seem to move like large waves or drones gushing through the Cathedral's massive interior.

Both recording sessions document a moment in the life of each site. They make for an honest portrait made up of complex and dense vibrations. Combining them took massive processing and delicate editing. The final installation of Conical Sound is like a cathedral, vertical and transformative. I was interested in focusing on each space's acoustic complexities.

All the recordings were done in stereo. With the output hardware I am using, Focusrite Scarlett 18i 20, I was able to collage the soundtracks and output them to a three-speaker system in a configuration that can accentuate the vertical cathedral by placing one side (right) very high and the other side (left) on the floor so that the shift of the left and right side can create an up and down effect, especially if it was experienced at the center of the installation. I am interested in developing a large-scale sculptural balloon sound bed (continuing my investigation of the tactility of sound started with my aluminum sound beds), placing the speakers near and facing in, directing the sound at them, taking advantage of resonance as well as filling the room with sound. A triphonic, as opposed to a quadraphonic, system seems to me, stronger, more direct and geometrically more solid. I also like how the three sound tower system symbolizes the Holy Trinity (both artists were Catholic), the three main verticals of Watts Towers, and the triangular geometry within the conical system.

Using sound, I want speak to the profound respect I have for both of these artists and their masterworks. I also want to create an experience that will be worthy of all of the support this project received both in the U.S. and in Barcelona. There are so many people to thank.

Conical Sound: Simon Rodia/Antoni Gaudi is a space that is filled with sound; sculpted and encompassing while conjuring a non-space, a place where listening is celebrated and architecture felt.

Lastly, I wanted to mention the childhood memory that started this whole idea. When I was a fourth grader at Wilton Place Elementary School in Los Angeles, in the library, I found a book with many pictures of Antoni Gaudi's work, including the Sagrada Familia. This would have been around 1974. I remember being awestruck by his work and the scale and color indicative of Gaudi. Not really understanding the chronology yet, I saw his work as a rip off of Watts Towers. Decades later, while researching both artists lives, I found out that Gaudi was unaware of Rodia but Rodia was often asked in lecturers if he had known Gaudi's work. Rodia was not aware of Gaudi's work and grew tired of this question. Conical Sound: Simon Rodia/Antoni Gaudi is my attempt to introduce them to each other.

ARTSREACH / UCLA : 1986-88

As I mentioned, when I was at the University of California Irvine for my Masters, one of our instructors was award-winning artist Linda Vallejo. I was her teacher's assistant for a semester. One day, she asked me if I would consider teaching in the prison system. She had taught through ArtsREACH and thought it would be a good experience for me. I taught drawing at the Men's facility in Norco, California and later a craft art class at the Women's facility in Chino, California.

At the start, as you might imagine, there was an interview and a security check and that took a while. Once I was cleared, I went to an orientation workshop where I got to meet artists who were already teaching at various facilities. In this group were artist Beth Thielen, who I would later work with at Metro, and poet Austin Straus, who was married to one of my favorite poets, Wanda Coleman.

I don't recall what the workshop consisted of but I felt fairly confident driving to the California Rehabilitation Center in Norco the following week for my first class. I was living in Gardena, CA at the time, commuting to UC Irvine and then driving to Norco about twice a week for about a year and a half. This trip was the beginning of my life-long back problem. The amount of driving and the stress on my body was too much for me but I still remember the somber rides home, late at night, after our drawing class with the inmates. The cold air through the opened window, music full blast, empty freeway and my nerves decompressing. The students were all amazing and accomplished people. Once they told me that the drawing class was the one thing they looked forward to each week. The class was a safe space for them, where they could drop their defense mode for a moment and be creative. Although there were classrooms for the dance, music and theater classes, they didn't have a room for us so we occupied a hallway. The class would start with all of us moving the tables and chairs into the hallway and then setting up for the assignment.

What was the most meaningful part of these classes for me was the discussion that would take place while we were drawing. Students would talk about their families, love relationships, incidents that happened that week, music, history, religion, you name it, we talked about it. While I was there, I never experienced lockdown, although the other teachers had stories. Lockdown is the moment the entire prison closes and no one can enter or leave until a security breech has been resolved. I heard it is a frightening experience.

We probably did two or three semesters and then I was asked to teach a class at the California Institute for Women in Chino. Specifically, the students I taught were inside a high security mini-prison within the institution. There, our classroom was guarded by a California Sheriff armed with a shotgun.

The students were continually leaving the class to get their medication. I was not allowed to bring any sharp objects into the institution so we primarily worked in oil pastels, vine charcoal or conte crayon. It was a rough experience for me. There was a policy that the inmates weren't supposed to talk about why they were incarcerated. However, I think because they were continually on medication, they wouldn't remember this policy, so unfortunately, they would tell me or allude to why they were in prison. It would just sort of slip as we were drawing. Sometimes I could stop them before it got to graphic but the stories that did get blurted out are images that I wish I didn't have in my mind.

Driving home, late at night on the open freeway, for long stretches, I would be the only car. I would always think about how just moments earlier we were all in a room making art and I was the only one who could drive home that night. The divide between us seemed mysterious and freedom was as thin as the briskness of the night air on the freeway.

PEACE RESONANCE: HIROSHIMA / WENDOVER

Peace Resonance is a multi-speaker audio presentation that links the Hiroshima Atomic Dome to the Wendover Hangar. It's about history, immigration, resilience and time. It's part of my on-going exploration about how we hear; sounds relationship to memory and the tactility of sound.

BACKGROUND
My family is from Fukuyama, Hiroshima, Japan. They immigrated to the USA in 1957. I was the first US-born family member and grew up with the "ghost" of their WWII history. As my art career grew so did my commitment to develop an artwork about our historical and personal connection to Hiroshima and the Atomic Bomb.

My first visit to the Hiroshima Atomic Dome was in 1988. I was a Monbusho Scholar, getting ready to begin my post-graduate studies in stage design at the University of Japan, School of Fine Arts. My Aunt, Grand Aunt and Grand Uncle brought me to the Hiroshima Peace Park, Museum and the Atomic Dome. It was an experience that took me years, if not decades to digest.

THE IDEA
Fast forward to 2014, I was visiting the Center for

Land Use Interpretations artist residency in Wendover, Utah (a former military base) and was struck by a large quonset across an airfield visible from where we stood. This Quonset at the end of the airstrip was the Wendover Hangar, where the Enola Gay B-29 Superfortress bomber flew out of, to fly to the Pacific and dropped the Atomic Bomb.

This experience led me to the conclusion that I really wanted to honor my family's history not in the shadows of war and destruction per se but rather in the current or re-built Hiroshima I experienced: reverent, contemporary and bustling. I was already conducting multi-point audio recordings of interior acoustics and presenting them in a kind of audio collage. These sound mash-ups are my attempt to address history, place and memory within a kind of audio omnipresent concept. I had just completed Conical Sound: Simon Rodia/Antoni Gaudi; a three-point audio recording of Watts Towers in Los Angeles and the Sagrada Familia in Barcelona, Spain; a kind of double-exposure of two interior acoustics.

What if I could conduct a three-point audio recording of the interior acoustics of the Hiroshima Atomic Dome, process that into an audio composition and then conduct that as a three-speaker performance in the Wendover Hangar.

It's also kind of like the monolithic mass in *2001: A Space Odyssey*, a mysterious mega-mass that returns to civilization, only to be discovered that it's a spacecraft that was launched by the US to accumulate data and was returning as a transformed mass of data.

I envisioned this as a conceptual voyage of the Enola Gay arriving back to the hangar seventy plus years later but carrying with it the redeveloped urban-scape of contemporary Hiroshima. It's a spiritual round trip. It's a metaphor of my American-ism and Japanese-ism, what it's like to be the child of immigrants, what it's like to be Japanese-American in post WWII America.

PERMISSION

It took a year to get permission to be able to record inside the Hiroshima Atomic Dome, a UNESCO Heritage site. I have a long list of individuals to thank but first and foremost would be Araceli Garcia, who was at the time with LA Mayor Garcetti's Office. She was able to get the Mayor to write a letter to Hiroshima's Mayor Matsui. This letter really got the ball rolling.

For the permission to record and then perform in the Wendover Hangar, a Smithsonian Heritage Site, also took a host of supporters to thank but most of all the Center for Land Use Interpretation played an instrumental role by introducing me to their contacts at the Wendover Airport.

DOCUMENTARY FILM

Through the support of Art Matters, NY, I was able to make arrangements to go to Hiroshima as well as hire videographer Tom Clancey, who traveled with me to Hiroshima, October 2016. He videoed my recording session in the Atomic Dome. He wasn't able to go with me to Wendover due to a schedule conflict. Luckily, Wengsan "San" Sit was available, who traveled with me to Wendover, Utah and documented the recording. Tom took all the footage of the two recording sessions and edited a short video that I've shown in conjunction with all the performances/presentations of this work.

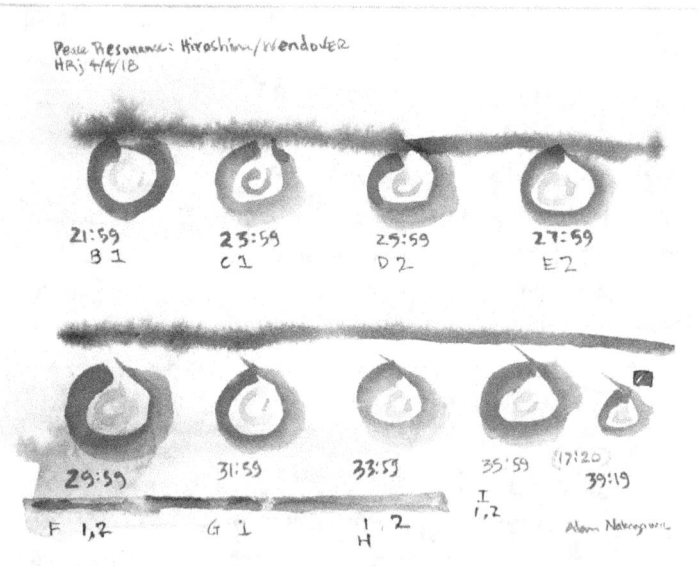

Peace Resonance: Hiroshima/Wendover Sound Map for Human Resources, 2018

PERSONAL NOTES:
The juxtaposition of different historical locations, their acoustic properties, the mash-up of those acoustics and how they represent a variety of his-

torical events is part of the equation of what drives these works. The other drive is the semi-autobiographical content. Collectively, these sites symbolize what it means to me to be Japanese-American in Post in post WWII US. The term multi-culturalism is a very popular topic but I gravitate more towards the term hybridity. Art has the luxury of being about the general and the specific simultaneously and my audio presentations are exactly that.

They are general in that they are about acoustic space and how sound is everywhere and that all space contains history. They are specific in that these spaces are personal sacred spaces. They represent my family's country of origin, their immigration and the unique elements of my geographical identity.

DEEP SPACE

my love for you is vast
so deep that it goes beyond my physical mass

in time; osmosis and continues to do so, an internal
arithmetic that I cannot control
is it the dark energy the theoretical physicists talk
about? 73% of the universe, still unknown
everything is not made up of atoms, the death of my
generation's paradigm

Einstein, in a letter to his niece, stated that the most
powerful force in the universe was love

What if dark energy is love?

Does it bother you that love is dark in this question?
It doesn't bother me. Rather, it feels quite accurate.

This would certainly explain the unmistakable
depth I feel for you.

I have never felt this before.

Is this string theory personified?

I don't need a large hedron collider, that costs bil-
lions of dollars, to prove this point. Like the Sagrada Familia, a construction project that has outlived
generations, I don't need to go beyond my existence.
It may not unravel the bolts locking an alleged path

to atom particles, a doorway to God, but we strive.

We build to reach and is that not love? the reaching within infinity?

Maybe what Einstein meant to say to his niece was that love is the infinity, the quantum computing promise of unimaginable algorithms.

The elevator at the end of Willie Wonka and the Chocolate Factory, the one with Gene Wilder, is that quantum computing? or is it a reality of transformation we currently cannot comprehend? and isn't that what makes us the unusual animal? that we strive to bridge the relationship between what we know and what we dream and what we cannot yet dream? And, isn't that why we love? Despite hearts crushed and emotional calluses built, we still hope. My goodness, what stamina! Isn't that why we demonize suicide? Because this dark matter, the truth of the universe is what we will, even within the most cerebral engineering, return to, love.

DREAM STATE AWAKE

Sleep Paralysis
I'll be reading in bed and sort of start dreaming and then the dream melds into what I am reading and then as I'm finishing a paragraph for instance, the dream is confusingly mixed up in what I read because I'll re-read some of it and none of what I thought I read is in the paragraph.

Once I had sleep paralysis, where I awoke but couldn't get up, move my limbs or speak. This happened a couple of years ago and then that week, they mentioned this phenomenon, on Radio Lab. I thought a spirit or ghost tried to inhabit my body like in the movies. It was freaky and wonderous.

In recent years, I've started dropping things I'm holding with one hand because I tried to grab something with my other hand while I'm thinking about something completely unrelated. I have dropped many things lately but only a few things have actually broken. This is one of the reasons I've been practicing Kinstuji lately, a Japanese folk-art where you celebrate the breaking of dishware by gluing it back together with a gold mixed glue.

From when I was little, up until around high school, once in a while, my sight would switch back and forth from what I was looking at in normal view to a close up and then back and forth, like that.

I would have to close my eyes and rest and then it would go away. I've only experienced this once since becoming an adult.

Sometimes, if I have a lot of alcohol, my vision gets super clear.

Sometimes in the morning, I would wake up and lay in bed and just start thinking but what I'm thinking is a continuation of what I was dreaming or what I thought I was just thinking about and all of a sudden it's a narrative and then I realize I must had fallen back to sleep but it feels like my eyes were open throughout this back and forth between awake and sleep.

(Wilton School playground experience playing on demoed basketball and volleyball poles)

ED.

there are educators and there are mentors

educators have the capacity to speak to a classroom full of students and voice information

mentors have the capacity to listen, ask questions and guide

when you meet an educator, they will assume you don't know so they may talk for a long time never asking any questions and end the exchange without knowing anything about you. their ok with that. They are casting a wide net in hopes that some of the students catch.

when you meet a mentor, they often start by asking questions and often they are searching for your passion button. Once they find it, they hope to ignite the conversation, understanding that a conversation is an exchange, both parties talking and listening to each other. From there, enrichment may occur, guidance and next-level thinking.

An educator assess by categorizing the person they are assessing. Of course, they can be very efficient but they are also limited to the number of categories they are pre-exposed to.

A mentor tries to understand the nature of someone

and therefore their individualism. They will keep digging until they feel they see a glimpse of true voice. Mentors are interested in also learning.

Sometimes, I am introduced to someone at a party and for some reason, they talk for fifteen to thirty minutes non-stop. On occasion, I have sat there listening for forty-five minutes to an hour. My sensitivity to sound and sound barrage is average but at some point, my retention dies. All sound is in addition to my pre-existing tinnitus so it's a collage. I'd say I can only really sit and listen to someone speak non-stop for five to ten minutes in terms of really digesting information.

Once I went on a three-hour road trip with someone who talked nonstop. When we got to where we were going, they talked most of the time with our mutual friend and then I drove back and they talked nonstop for another three hours. When I finally got home, I went straight to bed and couldn't do anything for two days.

In the 1980's, I read in Newsweek magazine that the military was already working on sonic weaponry. I understood that to be the ability to manipulate soundwaves into disabling or killing people.

When an earthquake occurs, the grand power of nature can be alarming but above and beyond the movement is the sub-sonic thrust our bodies absorb. This sudden and heighten disturbance can really affect us and is the key to why many find earthquakes so frightening.

I understood that at Guantanamo Bay, prisoners were tortured by having to live in 24-7 cell conditions of extraordinarily loud amplified sound and constant light. Partly sleep deprivation and part nerve torture, these prisoners eventually became zombie-like and will sign anything you put in front of them.

A SONG I SANG IN A DREAM THIS MORNING BOOK DROP

My soul was raised, by turtles and cranes
They told me not to reach, for riches or fame
Sometimes it feels, this is crumbling sand
Waiting for the pendulum, swing to drier land

My heroes are spirits, that point to the goal
But on my map, less yes's than no's
I know in my heart, all this could change
In the meantime, it's more of the same

(chorus)
Where are you now? Where are you now?
Where are you now my sweet, sweet love?
Where are you now? Where are you now?
Where are you now my sweet, sweet love?

Sometimes your lost, but your eyes still glow
Lived no regrets, but now they stand in rows
There's a rage that rings, that we once shared
Days that end, wondering if it's still there

~ 75 ~

(chorus)

> There's no rock won't move, norms once impossible
> Remember what you wished, start again your unstoppable

We're all waiting, for someone to lead
Is that the crop, that harvests no seed?
Where the dollar is god, no balance in sight
Where change is the dream, when will it take
flight

> (chorus)

CUTTING

Never telling you too close
Playing like there's a prize
Heavy like forgetting
Cutting the hand, you rely

I grab this and then do that
I drop what I had grabbed
I pick this up again
Synapses aging bad

> Hear there's one there, hear there's one
> there
> Lift me up where, above the sunshine
> Hear there's one there, another one
> there
> Lift me up where, they sing the last line

FIRST DATE AT SCOOPS

I fell in love with an amazing woman in Sayama, Japan in 1990.

Sayama is a small city in Saitama Prefecture. It's where the third most popular tea in Japan is grown. Iruma River flows through it. Tokyo is a forty-minute train ride away. It's where I really gained a sense of what it means to work with a community as an outsider.

And, it's where I met my ex-wife.

She didn't speak any English and I spoke very remedial Japanese but when you fall in love, that doesn't really matter. In retrospect, the fact that I had fallen in love with Japan and was at the tail-end of my scholarship there may had inspired me to propose to her. No, in truth, we had fallen in love. It marked the conclusion of a life changing experience, my first time in Japan and the end of my Monbusho Scholarship, researching Japanese Stage Design at Japan University School of Fine Arts.

She was charming, beautiful and we laughed a lot.

My ex-wife is a drummer and I am a drummer. Our first "date" was in a music studio going over a holiday swing drum chart she needed help with. We would often hold hands, listening to music, and squeeze each other's hand to the beat of the song. We were like two metronomes. In the end, thirteen years later with two kids and living in Los Angeles, she emailed me at work announcing she was leaving us to return back to Japan that coming Friday. At the time, we still lived together but it was the first time I heard from her for weeks if not months. It was the conclusion to a very slow downward spiral of our relationship; a majestic and numbing process of solitude oddity due to the deterioration of our communication.

The good news was the kids where going to stay with me.
The bad news was that she wasn't going to be with the kids.

Once she was gone, seven days after I received her email, I enrolled in therapy through my medical plan. The kids started therapy as well. It was so difficult, I don't remember most of it.

In truth, I was a zombie; continuing fatherhood, work and my art projects. I was in a trance but had every intent to do the best job I could while not really being 100% anywhere. I have to thank my friend and co-worker Jeff Mohr. Much younger than I, he had been introducing me to bands I was unaware of and the music of two bands he introduced to me in particular helped me transition through the levels of post break-up emotions; shock, anger, sadness and acceptance. The bands where the Shins and Death Cab for Cutie, masters at expressing love and depression.

The other media that helped me through this zombie phase was that each night I took in a solid dose of Comedy Central on cable television. In the 2000's, it was mostly one stand-up comedy show after another, especially late at night when my insomnia would be in full force.

There was no comedian I enjoyed more than Maria Bamford. I remember seeing her for the first time on TV, it was like the first time I saw Nirvana's Smells Like Teen Spirit video; I was a deer in headlights. Bamford's jump from child-like high pitch darkness to exaggerated adult caricature was an amazing vehicle for her zany-conclusive and highly neurotic narratives.

The nightly dose of the Shins, Death Cab for Cutie and Comedy Central was my cocktail of choice and it numbingly floated me through the first few years of post-marriage surrealism, which was much like a parade in a small town you've never been to at the pace of a Bill Viola slow motion art video.

A couple years later, one of my closest friend-couples told me they had met online and, although the idea repelled me at first, I decided to try it.

Have you tried this? You have to write about yourself, upload images of yourself and answer a bunch of questions which are supposedly going to help present you to a wide or not so wide array of potential partners who had to compile the same information for their profiles. It's harder than writing art grant applications.

What happens is that you become semi or completely obsessed with it. Every free and not-so-free moment, you check to see if anyone had been fooled enough by your page that they might want to say hello and/or anyone you said hello to might respond. It's a great example of how a system can manipulate your expectations and draw you into lock-step for the most basic social need; a digital meat market.

The truth is, I really loved my job, enjoyed being a single parent and had an art career that kept me busy but the void my ex-wife left became unbearable at times so online dating seemed like a good option.

One day, I got a message. I don't remember what it said but it doesn't really matter because I rarely got messages and getting any response was ultra-exciting. The image was of a woman in a blue business dress against a wall in an environment I read as a symposium for work. You couldn't really see her face. We exchanged messages for a while and it seemed to be going well and led to wanting to meet in person. I suggested Scoops Ice Cream on Heliotrope Avenue (which has since closed at this location), which is my favorite ice cream shop. It was founded by someone who went to CalArts and rather than becoming an artist, he became an ice cream maker.

Now mind you, I didn't really know what she looked like because her profile shot was her in a room, full body but a little far away from the camera. She was blonde and had an attractive style. Her texts were clever and insightful and funny. She said she traveled a lot for work so in my mind I thought she was in sales or some corporate job. She also mentioned that she had a skin problem and was self-conscious about showing a close up of her face. However, when we finally scheduled the first date, she did share her name, Maria.

Date One: It was at night, as I approached Scoops. The front door is glass and when I peered in, I saw the back of Maria sitting at one of the tables. As I opened the door to walk in, I remember thinking, "Wait a minute, is this Maria Bamford?" and it was. Now, I was already nervous for this first date but having that realization seconds before we met stunned me. Is it Medusa who freezes or turns anyone into stone who sees her? I'm not saying she's Medusa, I'm just trying to express what that thought did to me. I guess I am often my own Medusa.

We sat across from each other, eating ice cream and talking about this and that for maybe an hour. I have no idea if I said much because I was in shock but I didn't want to tell her I was fan. I thought that would not be cool so I tried my best to play it as if I had no idea about her being a comedian. I do remember thinking, "Wow, this is just like her stand up," because she spoke about some of the things she talks about in her show i.e. her Mother, growing up in the Midwest and her Sister and Brother-in-law. The only difference was that the entire time or more realistically, the entire show was in her actual voice. I remember thinking how magical it was to have a one-on-one experience of the shows I had been watching on Comedy Central. I guess it went well enough that we made a second date. I had mentioned the Henri Magritte exhibition at LACMA but she said no to that. "I'm not really into Magritte," she said.

She suggested the Rabbit Museum in Pasadena. I had never heard of it. The following week was Christmas and the couple whose home was the Rabbit Museum opened it up to the public on Christmas day. A week later, Christmas day, I'm at the Rabbit Museum with my favorite comedian, Maria Bamford. This can only happen in Hollywood.

I picked her up at her apartment, which is always a sign that some level of trust has been established, right? As we drove to Pasadena, the "show" continued and I loved it. The Rabbit Museum was dark like Death Cab for Cutie or the Shins and Maria was right out of Comedy Central and it was Christmas. I think that's all I need to say about that. It was too perfect. It was definitely better than the Magritte exhibition.

Afterwards, we were hungry but since it was Christmas, nothing was open. You know what's always open on Christmas? Canters Deli, so we drove across town for dinner to my beloved deli.

CANTERS: In high school, this was our hang. We didn't have much money so my friends would each order something minimal. I would always get a hot tea and a toasted plain bagel with cream cheese. We would sit there for hours and they would let us. I love that place.

CANTERS: I once dated an amazing woman for about a year. She hated Canters so for a year I didn't go there. When we broke up, the first place I went to was Canters. I was so happy to be back.

OK, back to the M. Bamford story: moments later, I'm at a crowded Canter's, eating my usual across from Maria Bamford, who by the way is super nice, educated, charming and extremely attractive. Her show continued as I ate my bagel and lox. The place was packed, obviously. It *was* Christmas after all.

When I dropped her off at her apartment, she said she could tell I was a good father but felt we had no chemistry and so that was that. Rejection is never easy but most of me didn't care that much about the conclusion of the date because I GOT TO SPEND CHRISTMAS WITH MARIA BAMFORD!!!!

About a week later, I sent her an email admitting that I was an actual fan of hers and appreciated her time. I never heard back from her, understandably. Every time I see her in an ad or on TV, I am rooting for her.

Since then, and it's been at least ten years, a friend of mine told me that he spoke with her at a party and that she and her husband are doing really well and that she's actually a super sweet person and I told him, yeah, I know.

I see this whole experience as if the Hollywood gods looked down at me and took pity on my situation and sent me an unbelievable gift, of which I will cherish for the rest of my life.

OBJECTS

I heard from someone that to understand the unit of a Nano, you have to imagine the speed in which your facial hair grows or something like that. I love that. I think about that every time I shave. Slow-mo. I like slow motion is the black and white photos of time.

I remember talking to Vera Rocha of the Shoshone/Gabrielino Nations. We were talking about dreams and I was telling her about this turtle image I dreamed of occasionally. Vera said that was my spirit animal. It's true I have always been drawn to turtles and tortoises. My practice can be described as gradual, maybe quiet and consistent. I like to build things one step at a time, repeat, repeat and at some point, a long time afterwards, it's this monumental endeavor, a collective object; cumulative.

My Father was a chef and owned two restaurants in his lifetime. For New Years, he would often create a Japanese traditional display of food for our family gatherings. Sometimes, there would be carved animals out of vegetables and almost always there would be a turtle and crane. They were the symbols of longevity and fidelity.

When I was a kid, I wanted to own a turtle. I saw them at the fish store. Little green turtles. I could watch them for hours. Unfortunately, there some disease or public scare about them. This would have been the early 1970's. All of a sudden, you couldn't find turtles at pet shops. Later, I heard that was some false information-based reaction, like MSG. By the time the turtles were for sale again, I had kids.

At Watts Towers, there are turtles in a pond and tortoises in a fenced area in the Garden. I love watching those guys. They are so magical to me. They weren't always there but now that they are, I may actually enjoy them more than I enjoy the Towers sometimes.

I don't like owning pets. I like animals but I have never had my own pet. Usually they were purchased or collected by someone else in the family. I've cared for a lot of animals because often, those who want pets never end up taking care of them. I ended up caring for them, even though that was never my intention. I don't think I like the responsibility or maybe it's the idea of owning a living being? I don't know what that says about me.

On the other hand, I do collect things, objects. Objects tend not to die. Not like a pet. I have a lot of stuff in my home. The vast majority of things I own are for art making or research or inspiration.

One of my cherished objects is a shaver. It's an old single silver razor type where you twist the handle to open or close the razor holder. It's not easy to find the single razors anymore. This razor was my Grandfather's. I remember after he died, his razor was in his medicine cabinet still. No one was using it so I took it. I used that for a long time. I traveled with it. I even got it professionally cleaned and tuned up once.

One year, I went to visit my friend, experimental theater Director Mallory Catlett, in New York. I stayed at her and Brian's apartment for a couple of nights. We had a great time that summer. However, when I got home the razor was missing. I had always had problems with going through TSA with shaving razors. Often, they confiscate my single razors. My mind instantly went to the airport staff as the culprit of my missing razor but soon I found out I left it at Mallory's when it came in the mail. That week, I went and bought a similar razor and stopped traveling with my Grandfather's. It is now framed and hangs in my studio.

In 1989, in the middle of my research scholarship in Japan, I came back to Los Angeles. On that short trip back, I went to visit my Grandfather, who was bed ridden at that time. I had heard he had been sick but I didn't know how bad it was. It turned out he was dying. This tank of a human being had turned fragile and sick. It completely ripped my equilibrium to see him like that. He seemed happy to see me which made me tear up. He could sort of still speak but it was very faint as I recall. He signaled with his hand to come closer and whispered for me to give him a shave.

I was like *absolutely*! I rushed to the bathroom,

grabbed his razor, a can of shaving foam and a wet towel. I was back in his room very instantly.

Now, I had never given anyone a shave before. My Grandfather's skin had turned wrinkled not unlike a turtles neck. It was not easy but I did the best i could. He seemed pleased. I stayed with him for a bit and left that day. He passed away shortly after that. It was the last thing or maybe I can say the final thing I did for him. Now his razor is in a frame.

OCTOBER 5, 2017

to asher hartman & tim reid (riting):
re: sorry atlantis, eden's achin' organ seeks revenge,
asher hartman, machine projects,

(Asher asked me to write my thoughts on his production and this is on his website)

october 5, 2017, an hour after experiencing: *sorry atlantis, eden's achin' organ seeks revenge (at Machine Projects in Echo Park)*, I was in my studio, typing this descriptive of my emotional summary having seen asher hartman's new work. these are not about the totality of the work but rather glimpses of parts of the 90-minute poem, their patina or like details for a diagnosis;

first and foremost, i was still buzzing. my blood, still bubbling like seltzer water, but thicker of course and not red but that color it is before it hits oxygen. my body feels like it's shifting between dimensions but it's not that it's unstable but rather in between affected and effected. everything is articulated, sharp and layered but in the way it is in dyslexia.

major imprints of tonight's performance/installation; narrative is a misnomer; pop referential is a solid strategy; relativity; maybe the supernatural; attention deficit disorder is society's cultural framework; our collective psychosis is a plane we share; a space that is language and we can comprehend its non-linearity as the true order of time; where poetry must evolve to; that which is effective, revealing and revelatory; experience is data and data is experience; the age of dysfunctional-ism with neither good or bad connotations; emotions are perfunctory and malleable; superficiality is dangerous but the true danger is when we read it superficially, when in fact, it has great depth and movement; relationships are amorphic and maybe we should approach them more like archeologists and not like real estate agents. maybe this will all look different in the morning?

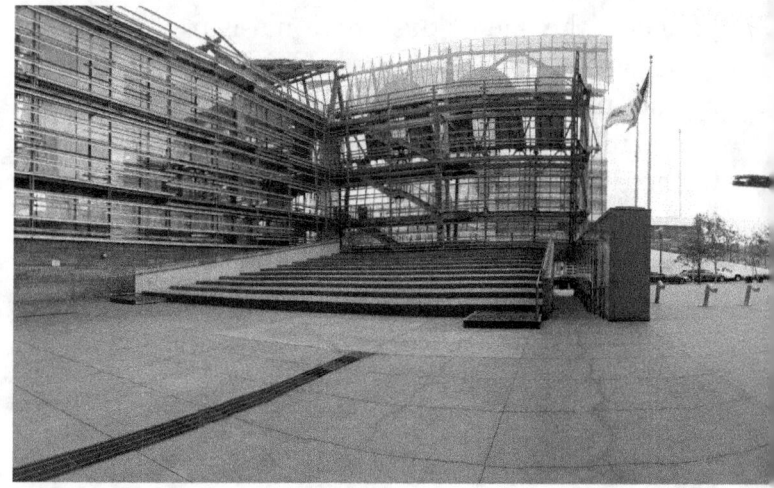

Caltrans Building/ LADOT offices, 100 Main Street, L.A. CA

LADOT CREATIVE CATALYST ARTIST IN RESIDENCE/ ARTIST NOTES

Alan Nakagawa
August 6, 2017

I'd like to try to articulate my experience as the first Creative Catalyst Artist in Residence (March 2016 through July 2017) for the City of Los Angeles' Department of Transportation as administered by the Department of Cultural Affairs.

First, I think it's important to state where I was in my career and my mind space at the time of the award. It was a national call and I responded to the application along with many other artists.

A L.A. native, I was trained in art administration at the Social and Public Art Resource Center in the early nineties. I co-founded the non-profit Collage Ensemble Inc., which I participated in its L.A.-centric inter-disciplinary/inter-ethnic arts collaborations from 1984 till it dissolved in 2011.

I managed public art projects for the L.A. Metro from 1992 through 2016. I curated Ear Meal webcast from 2010 to 2016, an attempt to document the multi-generational cast of the L.A. experimental music and sound art community. Those are the key ingredients that led me to the moment I applied for the A.I.R. at LADOT.

Starting in 2008, my solo art path began to build momentum. By the time (2015) the Call for the LADOT opportunity was sent to me, I was attracted to it but also at the time, I was asking for a "sign," a type of nod from the "universe," to say to me, "Time to leave Metro and pursue the elusive title of Full-time Artist."

I've told this story many times; when I got the call that I was chosen, I knew it was time to make that career decision. I let Metro know about the award and it came back that it would be a conflict of interest to remain at Metro and receive this A.I.R. Metro wanted me to not take the award. I thought about it for a few days and then one morning, I walked into Maya Emsden's office, Director of Metro Art, who I had worked with through thick and thin since 1992 and asked her if she had a minute. I closed the door, which worried her a bit and we both sat down. I opened with, "I always wondered what this day would be like"… I don't think you could have had a more heartfelt interaction. We worked together for twenty-four years. That's a long time. Suffice to say, I had as much "training" as one could possibly have in order to take on this new A.I.R. honor.

Before the contract was signed, I was already being asked to participate in meetings with folks at LADOT and also with outside organizations involved in Vision Zero (an international campaign to eliminate traffic fatalities). It was my crash course in the intricacies of this International movement. First, decreasing the rising numbers of traffic fatalities by 20% by the end of 2017 and two, bringing it down to Zero in the future.

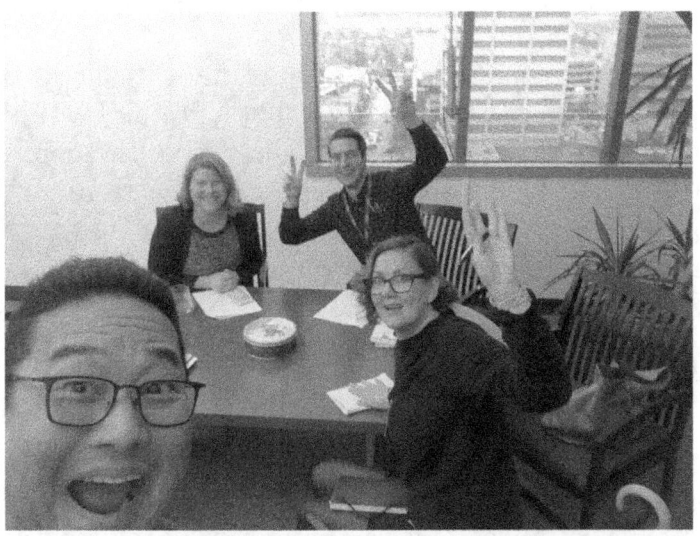

L-R; Nakagawa, Seleta Reynolds, Nat Gale, Danielle Brazell

Before I continue with my LADOT orientation, I should also mention how this A.I.R. opportunity came into being. As I understand it, Danielle Brazell, Cultural Affairs General Manager, and Seleta Reynolds, LADOT General Manager, were selected by Mayor Garcetti and sworn in at the same City Council Meeting, where they met for the first time. They discovered that they were kindred spirits and agreed that if an opportunity arose, they would love to collaborate on a project. Following that encounter, Cultural Affairs conducted a think tank for new opportunities the Department could venture to bring art into the City. One idea was an artist in residency in every City department, ala Mierle Ladderman Ukeles and the New York City Department of Sanitation. Since Danielle had already had a positive relationship with the new GM for LADOT, she extended the premier offer and Seleta agreed.

The reason this is so important is that the buy in is from the top down, if you will. I don't think I would have been so successful if I didn't have the confidence that Seleta and Danielle gave me from day one. It's because they instilled a level of confidence in me that I felt open to listen and then dream big but realistically for what is a very short period of time (twelve months) to develop art enhancements/projects in a culture that is not used to incorporating the arts.

The scope of the contract was $20,000 to cover artist fee, insurance , taxes and minor project expenses for one year. I participated in brainstorming sessions with Cultural Affairs and Ciclavia which resulted in an application for a National Endowment for the Arts grant. Months later we would find out that we would not receive that award. It would have continued the A.I.R. a second year. However, the exercise of collaborating on the grant application was helpful because I got to meet the team, begin to understand the community players and it made me focus on the philosophy of how we were going to build this Creative Catalyst A.I.R. position.

Here's what was in my contract:

"…. The Creative Catalyst will use a three-step process to leave a lasting legacy of art, design and culture at LADOT.

The processes three steps:
☐ Research
☐ Develop
☐ Use

…1. Fully document the three-step process…

…2. Interview no fewer than ten (10) LADOT employees…

☐ Attend any internal LADOT meetings….
☐ Submit a minimum of six (6) articles for LADOT's website/blog…
☐ Use social media as often as possible….
☐ Produce two (2) or more art pieces about Vision Zero and/or LADOT
☐ Facilitate no less than three (3) public classes or workshops with members of the public and LADOT staff on the progress of their work:
☐ Engage Los Angeles residents, visitors, civic and elected leaders, young people, adults….about the

importance of Vision Zero….. "

In addition, I was asked to:
- [] Recommend a path forward for an internal art program/strategy for LADOT
- [] Support the transition phase for the next AIR "

My main contact, support and friend during this entire A.I.R. was Nat Gale, the LADOT lead for Vision Zero. Without Nat, none of this would have been possible. Not only could he make things happen, he also created a culture of collaboration and excitement that rubbed off on each team person. Of course, I am sure everyone believed in the objective of the campaign but it sure helps to have a positive, innovative and productive lead. From the first team meeting, it was obvious to me that each member was handpicked. It was and is a dream team. Each person brought years of experience in her/his/their field and engaged in their daily work as a problem solver and team builder. It was inspiring to work with this team and made my work that much more fun and rewarding.

Here's a summary of the projects I instigated during the twelve months of this residency:

L.A. DOT POD
I really didn't know about LADOT's history or culture. How the heck was I going to hit the ground

running and be effective within a Vision Zero team already in full swing?

I asked Seleta Reynolds, LADOT General Manager and Nat Gale, LADOT Vision Zero lead, for a list of a dozen folks who I could conduct oral histories of. They could be either currently at LADOT or retired. A few names were already repeating in my meeting with staff, i.e. Frankie Banerjee, John Fisher, Zaki Mustafa.

I was able to utilize my experience as an oral historian and sound artist by engaging in a meaningful dialogue with these amazing professionals and edit these down to short podcasts. My background as a composer enabled me to record a series of transition music specific for this series and also avoid any copyright issues.

For the first three months, I mainly met with staff, participated in Vision Zero internal and external meetings, conducted oral history sessions and edited those sessions into podcasts. The podcasts were uploaded onto Soundcloud and the staff built a Creative Catalyst page on the Vision Zero website where anyone could access the podcasts. There were enough to call it a collection, which I titled L.A. Dot POD, LADOT's first podcast station.

What L.A. Dot POD does as a collection is give a first-hand account of the development of the Los Angeles transportation system. It also begins to humanize the agency by presenting the voices and experiences of individuals who played a key role in the agency's development. Each conversation mentioned how LADOT had been transitioning from a car orientation to a people orientation.

STORYTELLING
In the midst of conducting the oral histories, it became obvious that the candid interviews were unique, educational and entertaining: the power of storytelling.

What's the value of storytelling in the Vision Zero message? Could it be beneficial to include storytelling in what was at the time a solely data-driven presentation?

I asked if I could produce a storytelling workshop for the key engineers working on Vision Zero? They said yes and I reached out to Gary Buchler, L.A. Producer of the Moth Story Hour and Shoot 'Em Up, a movie script development workshop. The Moth Story Hour is a nationally syndicated radio show about storytelling. Gary was very accommodating and brought Moth Grand Slam Winner Jessica Lee Williamson to a room full of traffic engineers. The storytelling workshop was excellent but what really floated the truth to the surface was the Q&A session immediately afterwards. Engineers are trained to be objective. Storytelling goes against that training because it's subjective. When Seleta and Nat said that they would like everyone to realign the task at hand with the stories behind the data, changing their methodology, it felt like a door was opened to the team.

DRAWING ON PUBLIC TRANSPORTATION

My studio is in Koreatown. When there was a LADOT meeting, I would ride my bike to the Metro Wilshire/ Western Station, take the train to Civic Center Station and ride to 100 Main Street (LADOT). While on the train, I would secretly draw my fellow transit riders. I was given a cubicle in the Vision Zero office area on the 9th floor. I used it as an art gallery and posted these drawings along with images of my AIR process. I started posting these drawings online too and that led to an invitation from art group, Slanguage, to display them at LAX Art Gallery in Hollywood.

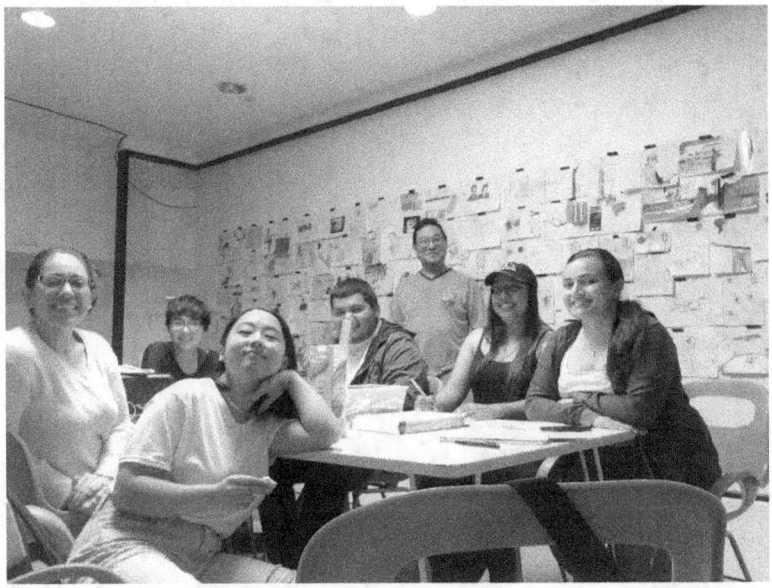

Nakagawa visits a Slanguage art workshop during his drawing exhibition at LAX ART, Hollywood CA

GHOST BIKES L.A.

One of the first things the Vision Zero team introduced me to was ghost bikes, which I hadn't known about before. Specifically, they told me about Danny Gamboa who is one of the leads of Ghost Bikes LA. No one at LADOT had ever contacted them so it felt right to bridge that gap.

The first time I met Danny and his crew, we hit it off. Danny has an art background, so we had some common language. That was important because they were a little reluctant to meet someone from the "City," since it's the "City" that usually takes the ghost bikes down. That is to say that the ghost bikes are in response to a bicycle fatality. The crew gets a bike, strips it and paints it all white, like a ghost. They then, often, illegally lock the bike up to the nearest street post at the crash site. Often, someone complains about the bike or it may be in the way of pedestrian foot traffic, so the City comes and takes the ghost bike away.

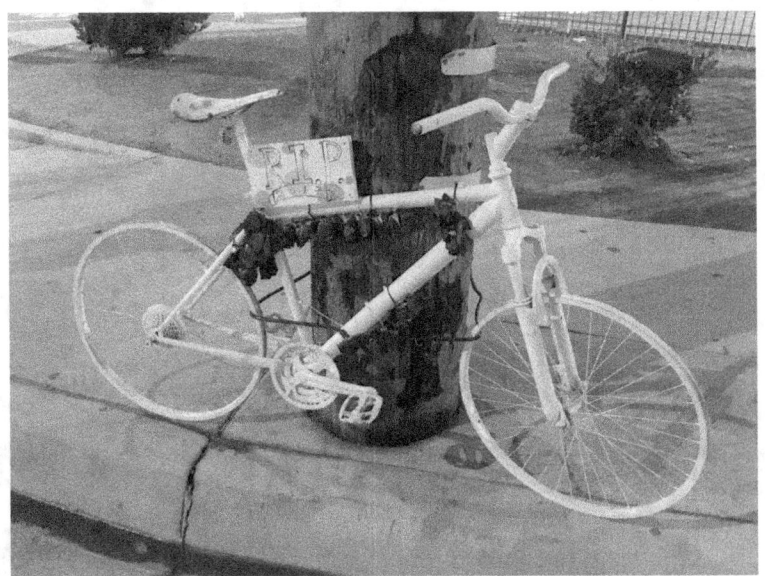
Ghost bike in Willowbrook CA, Ghost Bikes L.A.

My first ghost bike experience started by getting a message that the fatal crash had happened, killing a bicyclist and the place and time that the crew would meet. After several of these and unfortunately there are a number of these a month, I was invited to join the crew which means that I was added to the secret Facebook page. Even after my LADOT residency, I have proudly continued to participate as a member of Ghost Bikes LA.

NEIGHBORHOOD JUSTICE PROGRAM
City Attorney Mike Feuer has instigated a restorative justice pilot project called the Neighborhood Justice Program. Simply, it's a way for first time misdemeanors to get that off their record by participating in a community support process. I was invited

into this program through City Attorney staffer and artist Carmelo Cruz.

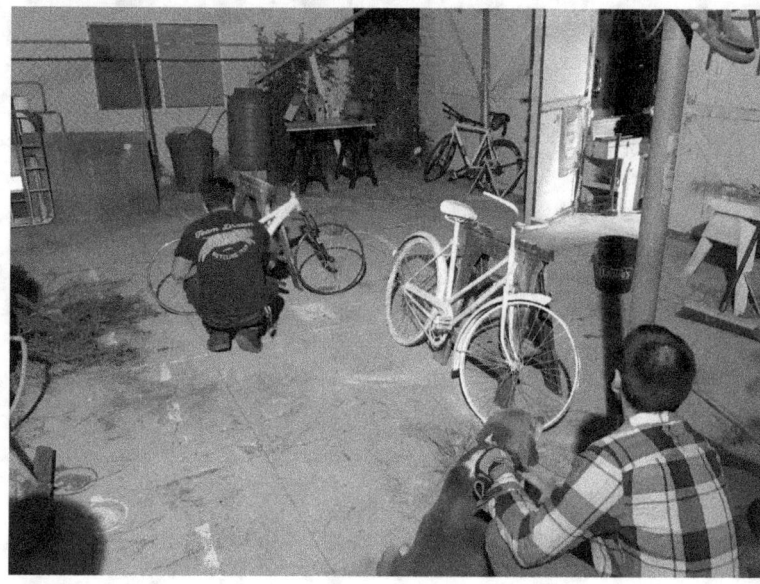

NJP participants supporting Ghost Bikes LA by painting donated bikes white at Nakagawa's studio in Koreatown L.A.

I've since become a member of their committee and when a participant fulfills all of their requirements, has either an art or bicycling interest, they can get assigned to me for their community hours. I have hosted several of these participants and they have joined me at my studio to prepare a ghost bike.

VISION ZERO FACEBOOK
Early on, the team made me one of the contributors of the Vision Zero Facebook page. That became one of my platforms to report to whoever was interested, what my residency was and what I was experi-

encing. It was great to upload pictures of meetings, inside the building we were in, which was designed by Thom Mayne.

WORLD DAY OF REMEMBRANCE
Halfway though the residency, during a Vision Zero Alliance meeting, Emilia Crotty of LA Walks, a non-profit organization promoting walking in neighborhoods, pulled me aside and asked if I'd be interested in doing something for World Day of Remembrance, an international day to remember those who have been killed in traffic.

I pulled together a committee including representatives from Vision Zero, Ciclavia, Metro, LADOT, LA Walks and Ghost Bikes LA and introduced them to Stephen Van Dyke, the lead of L.A. Road Concerts. Stephen organizes these one-day guerilla performance/installation events along the entirety of a street in Los Angeles, i.e. Sunset Blvd from one end to the other or Mullholland.

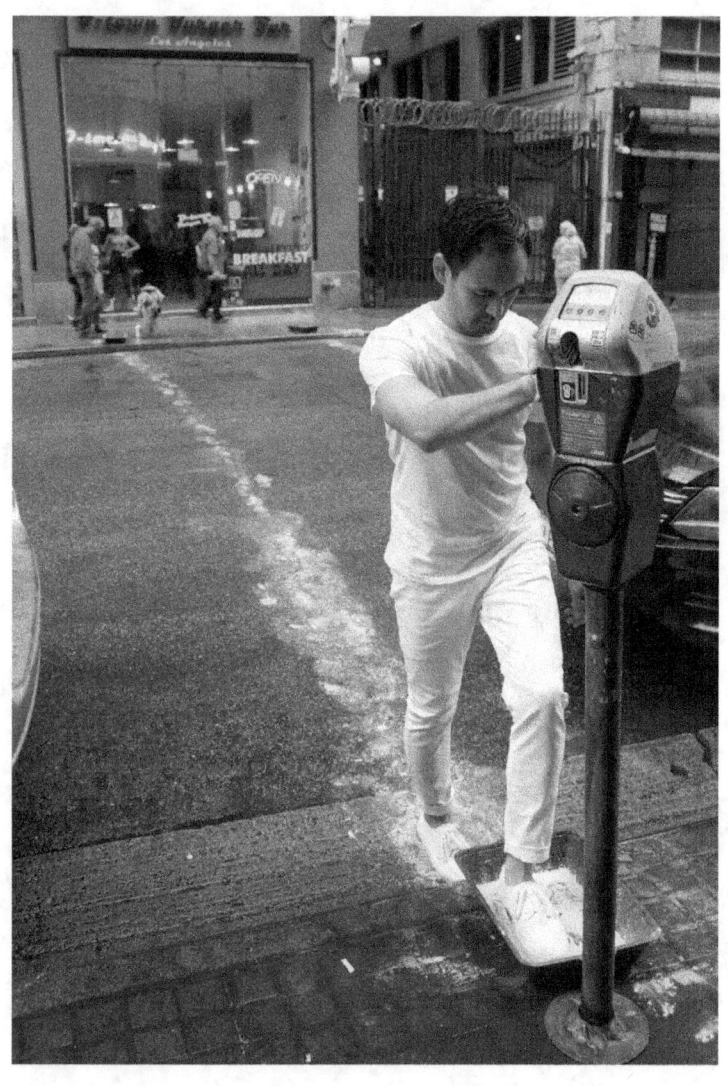

"Desire Lines," Michael Rippens, World Day of Remembrance, 2016

We only had six weeks to pull it off. The day was November 20, 2017 and we were able to get over thirty artists/artist teams to present along Spring Street and Main Street in Downtown Los Angeles during a span of four hours. From performance art to dance and computer music to a New Orleans style procession, audience and residence witnessed two streets of colorful surprises, all commemorating traffic fatality in Los Angeles.

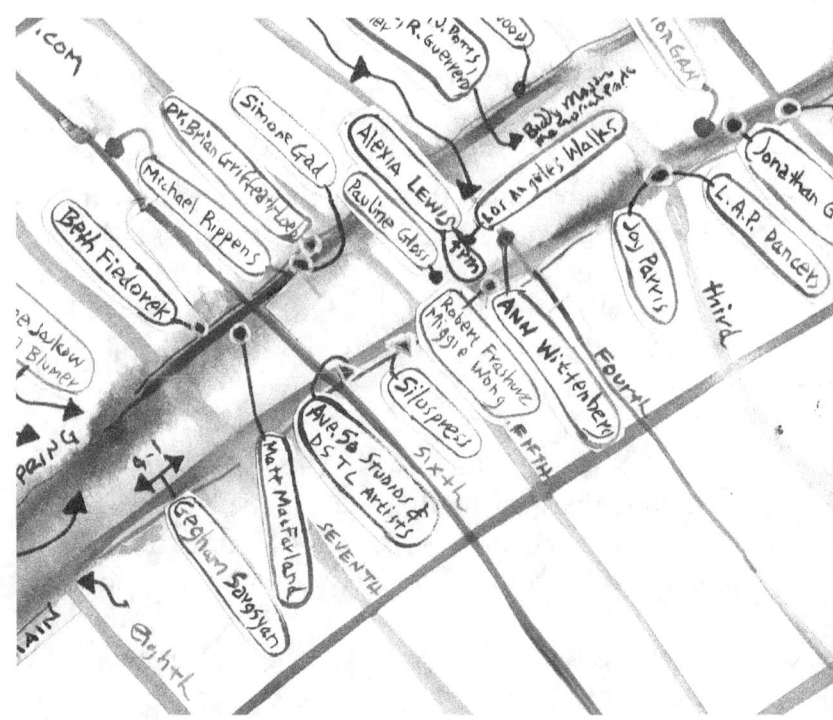

Map for 2016 World Day of Remembrance

L.A. DOT ZINE 1.0
(Caffeine Tour)
One day, the Vision Zero staff invited me to go

with them to the City Print Shop to review the test print of the Vision Zero brochure. I had never been there. It's located at the Piper Tech Building at Vignes and Santa Fe Avenue in the Northeast area of Downtown LA. (ironically across the street my former Metro office). It's a gigantic four-story building with no windows and spans the footprint of three city blocks. The print shop is half of the second floor. In this vast room is the history of printing. In the back they have letterpress machines and, in the front, they have several four-color printing machines, in the midst are a binding section, shipping area, offices, a CNC studio, etc. Needless to say, I was drooling. I met the managers and as was always the case, introduced as the City's artist in residence. I think they could tell I was excited so they gave me a tour of the facility, at the end of which I asked if they would want to work with me on a project and they smiled and said yes.

That's when I came up with the zine idea. I've been making zines for many decades but by hand. Zines are often very DIY, personal little magazines about very specific topics, and have become very popular.

For Vision Zero, I curated a zine that included poems, photography, drawings and Ghost Bike documentation. The topic was loosely about pedestrian rights and traffic. I asked a handful of my friends to donate a piece which they generously did and I crafted a small zine which the Print Shop digitized, printed and bound. At first, I asked for 500 copies, which is way more than I ever make on my own but they seemed to be confused by this quantity. Somehow, the Print Shop eventually talked me up to 5,000, which is still way lower than the typical quantity they are used to producing. In the long run, the zine was a hit and Vision Zero staff began to use it as a giveaway at the community events. Artist Audrey Chan, Metro Little Tokyo Station Artist, said that it may very well be the most printed zine in the world and actually exceeds the quantity of most published books.

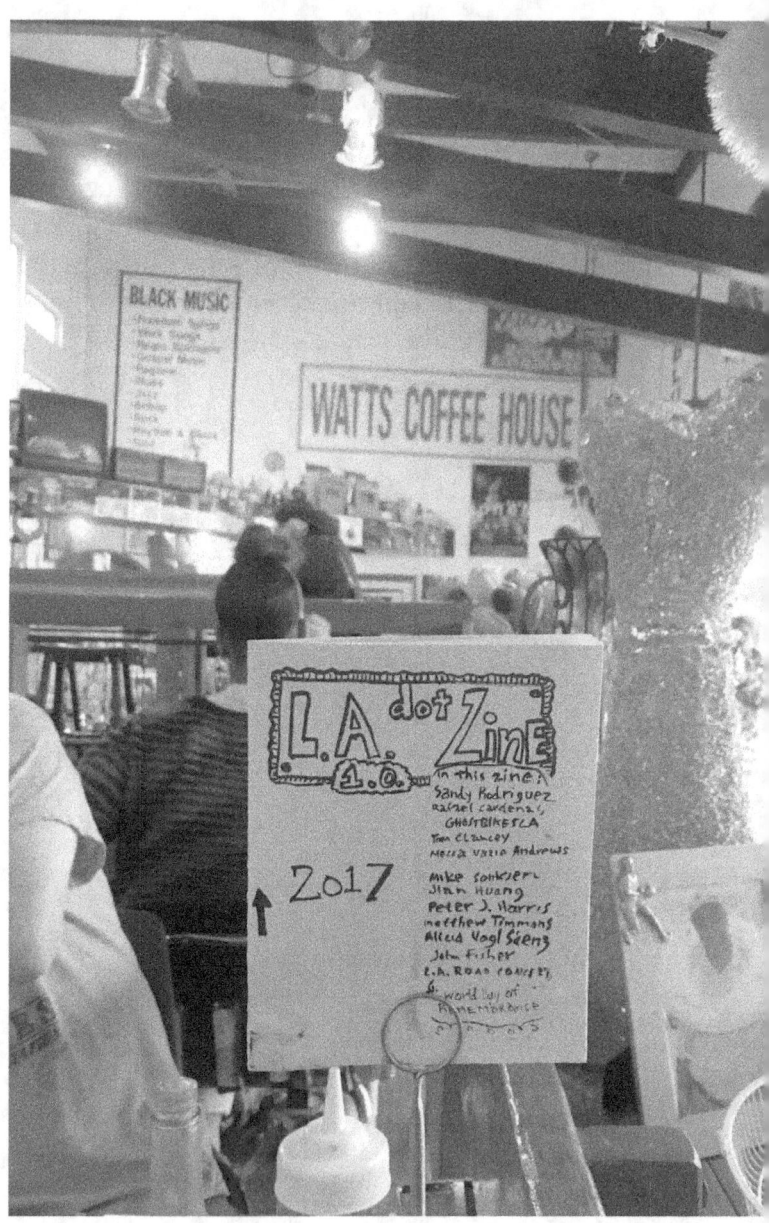

Watts Coffee House-Caffeine Tour/L.A. Dot Zine 1.0, Nakagawa, 2016

CAFFEINE TOUR

The City of L.A. is divided into fifteen Council Districts. In most of these districts, there are hot spots for traffic fatalities. I thought I could pick a coffee shop in each district and do a performative action using social media. I called this the Caffeine Tour. For three weeks, I would spend an hour at a coffee shop, wearing my LADOT safety vest, with a stack of the zines at the corner of the table, I would order a beverage and some snacks and try to introduce myself to those sitting around me. A few times, people would ignore me but the majority of times, I would find someone who was curious enough to engage in a conversation with me. Once I spoke to one person, inevitably others would be open to at least taking a zine. After my one hour, I would leave a stack of zines and announce on social media that there's a stack of free art zines at such and such coffee shop. I ended up performing eighteen of these actions. We also donated 500 zines to the L.A. Public Libraries Teenscape Program.

ECHO PARK FILM CENTER A.I.R.
(Speed Kills)

At one of the Vision Zero meetings, we were brainstorming about the various ways we could artistically present the issues of traffic fatalities at community events. Projecting images was discussed and I suggested animation would be a good way to symbolically tell the story of traffic safety and fatalities.

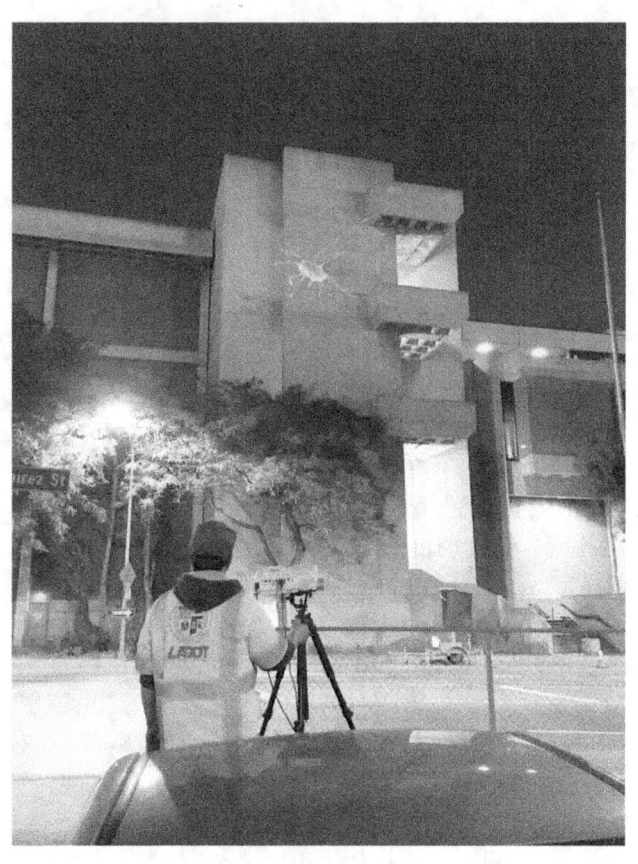

Nakagawa projecting SPEED KILLS in Downtown L.A., 2017

For a couple of weeks, everyone reached out to friends in the animation field but with no luck. Serendipitously, I received an email from Echo Park Film Center (EPFC) regarding their artist in residency program. In this residency, they team you up with a filmmaker and provide a small budget for you to complete a small project. I wrote a proposal where I could learn the basics of animation and create a work to support my A.I.R. at LADOT. I was awarded the EPFC A.I.R. and for two months, worked with Gina Napolitan of EPFC, learned a program called Dragon Frame and hand drew the artwork for my animation. The end result is a short black and white animation called "SPEED KILLS."

One evening, with assistance from L.A. photographer Elon Schoeholz, we drove around in my truck which I equipped with a laptop, projector and gas-powered generator. On various walls that overlooked the freeways, that surround Downtown LA, we projected SPEED KILLS for about ten minutes. A documentary of this exercise is online and was presented as my final project at EPFC.

MAR VISTA GREAT STREETS PROJECT

The last quarter of my A.I.R. was focused on the Mar Vista Great Streets project, a mile corridor on Venice Blvd between Beethoven Ave (near Venice High School) and Inglewood Avenue (Mar Vista Library). I remember in the meeting that Seleta Reynolds said she wanted me to focus on this project, Nat Gale commented that they were almost done and asked if this was really a good idea to introduce me so late in the schedule. At times like this, I try to be quiet and watch the navigation of concerns. They concluded that I would go to a couple of the weekly multi-departmental meetings, not say anything, and report back to Nat with what I thought our options were.

So, these weekly meetings were a bit intense. That

is to say, the air in those meetings was so thick, you could cut it with a knife. Later, I would find out that there had been a lot of "challenges" with the schedule regarding delivery dates and construction, which is often problematic. They had a lot of stop and starts. Basically, there was tension between the community, government offices and City departments. I wasn't convinced, like Nat said, if this was a good idea but I had been working on some art strategies and decided that it might be a good fit to modify them for this corridor in Mar Vista. They were retrofits in nature to the project and pilot projects. "Retrofits" and "pilot projects" are terms I learned while at Metro and they tend to be very friendly to project teams in government.

I'd like to also point out that I was no stranger to this corridor. First of all, the Social and Public Art Resource Center, where I was trained in the 80's, was a mile west of this area. On this corridor is Mitsuwa Market, a Japanese market. Next door to Mitsuwa, there used to be Hakuyoshya Cleaners. My mom was the manager of that store for eight years. Both my kids played and practiced basketball at Venice High School, Webster Middle School and Mark Twain Middle School through the Asian League and as players of the Culver City High School teams, schools along or next to this corridor. Lastly, south of the corridor on Centinela Avenue is Angel Maid Bakery, which my daughter and son-in-law co-own.

The advantage of me entering this project at the tail end of coordination is that the community contacts were already fairly well established so I took advantage of the Mar Vista Artwalk committee and was introduced to Lenore French, a local activist and community organizer.

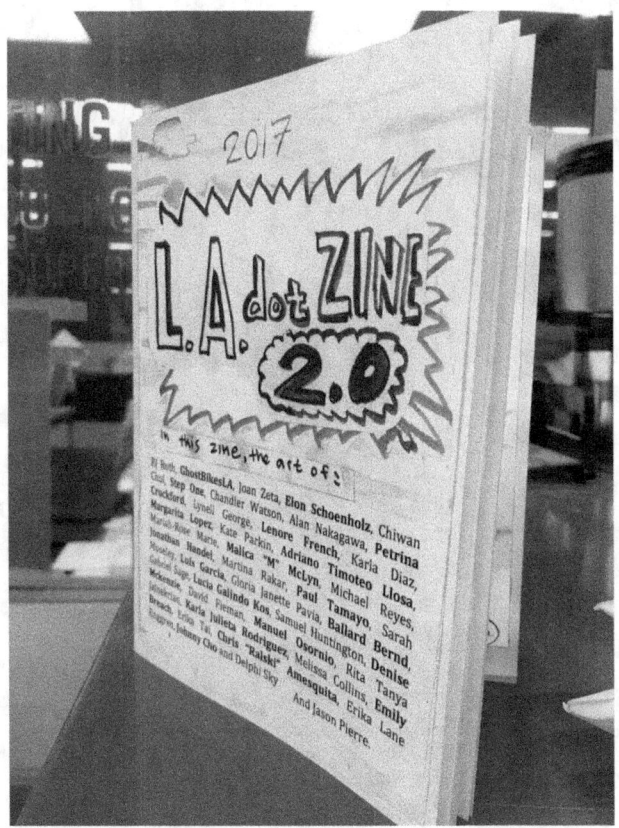

L.A. Dot Zine 2.0

The Mar Vista Great Streets Public Art Project had three components;

1) "LA Dot Zine 2.0"; Lenore introduced me to the local poetry association, Philosopher's Stone. I wrote a call for members to donate one haiku about traffic safety or pedestrian rights. We ended up getting thirty submissions. Lenore also got some of the local visual artists to donate work as well. I added a handful of LA-based artists and poets. This became LADOT's second artist zine. We donated 1,000 copies to the Mar Vista Public Library and again 500 to the L.A. Public Libraries Teenscape Program. The rest were distributed by LADOT's Vision Zero team.

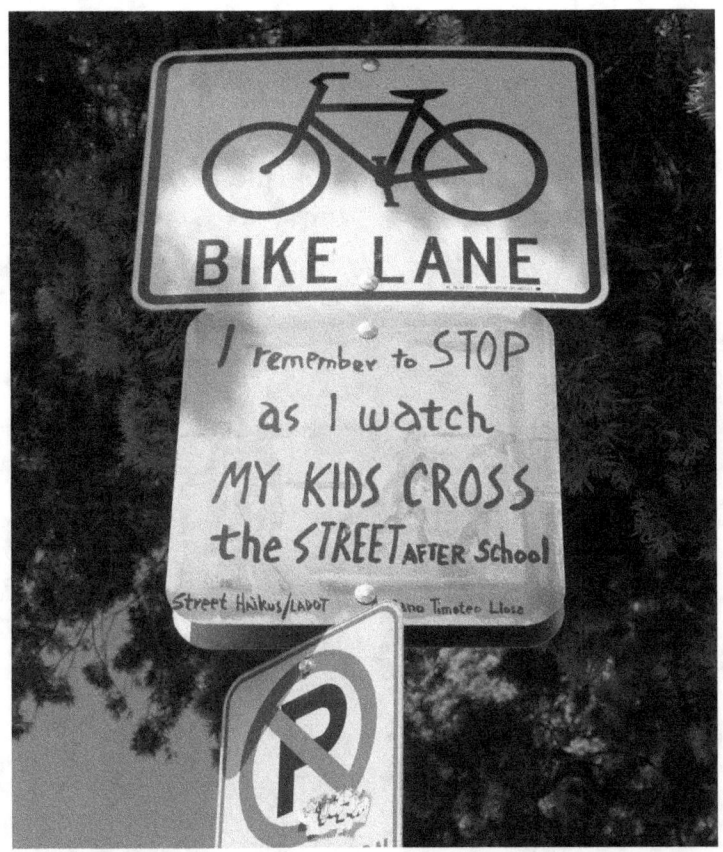

One of thirty-six Street Haikus on Venice Blvd. L.A. 2017

2) "STREET HAIKUS"; I took all the haikus and created paintings. I created high resolution files of these paintings and asked the City Sign Shop to create an 18" x 18" street sign of each. There are eighteen Bike Lane signs along this Venice Blvd. corridor. We had thirty-six haikus. I asked permission to install two haikus on each bike lane post, one facing traffic and one facing the opposite direction.

I explained that this was symbolic of LADOT's shift from an engineering for car traffic orientation to an engineering for people safety orientation. The LADOT Westside Engineering Department and Facilities worked on the implementation and installation and by the end of July 2017, thirty-six STREET HAIKUS were installed up and down Venice Blvd.

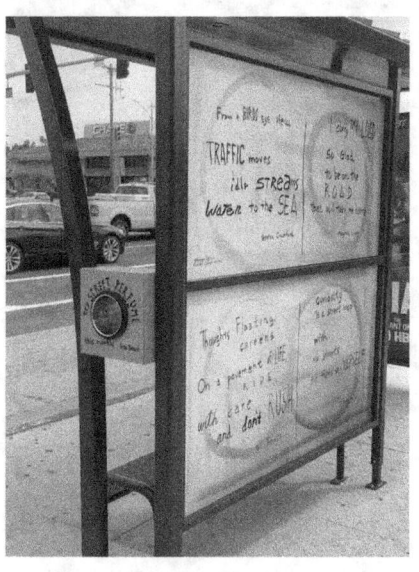

Street Perfume Bus Stop, Venice Blvd. and Centinela Ave. L.A. 2017

3) "STREET PERFUMES"; early on, LADOT staff Valerie Watson was explaining to me that she wished there was a way to change the public perception of streets. After that conversation, I toured the streets of Downtown L.A. and was amused by how many different smells there were, some pleasant and some not. I thought, if we could change the smell of this

experience, that would, at the very least, open the conversation to how we perceive the urban environment. I had learned about a non-profit organization in Chinatown called the Institute of Art and Olfaction. I signed up for some classes and soon was nose deep into perfumery. I am still a novice but I learned enough to be able to create three perfumes or STREET PERFUMES. I began to research how we could spray this into the streets and found that it was too expensive to build a machine. I did find some machines online but none of them seemed industrial enough to withstand the wear and tear of the public space.

Again, serendipitously, Danielle Brazell had had a meeting with Francois Nion of JCDecaux. They have the contract for bus stops throughout the City. Francois said he wanted to work on art projects and asked Danielle how could Cultural Affairs help make that possible? Danielle recommended he and I meet and at that first meeting, I told him about my Street Perfumes and he offered a perfume machine that was left over from a previous perfume ad in Chicago they had produced. What luck!

On the Mar Vista corridor, at Venice Blvd and Centinela Ave. is a JCDecaux bus stop. We installed the perfume machine there and I designed artwork for both sides of the main wall. One side included four of the thirty-six Street Haikus and the other side was an explanation of all three components of the Mar Vista Great Street Public Art Project, including descriptions of the three Street Perfumes.

For four months, June, July, August and September 2017, the Street Perfumes rotated in the machine. The machine is a box with a chrome cylinder. There's a motion sensor so that if you put your hand in the cylinder, a short sprit of perfume sprayed your wrist. I wish this project could have continued for longer but the box was not engineered to last more than a month. The maintenance crew had to show up regularly to reset the mechanism in box so that it would spray correctly. This was over and beyond any acceptable amount of maintenance so we had to take it down. Having said that, it did average 500 uses a month.

LADOT Creative Catalyst A.I.R. SUMMARY
I was so honored and grateful for this unique opportunity. It was in many ways, a chance to exercise all these creative muscles I've been trained in for the past three decades. It was a unique and brilliant experience. I only hope that the department and the people I worked with got half as much out of it as I did. I know I'll carry what I've learned at LADOT with me to the next project(s).

The team introduced me to many of the sections in the department and it was fairly clear who was supportive and who were cautious but there were far more who were supportive. After all, LADOT had never had an artist on staff so there was a level of doubt and suspicion. One staff clearly stated to me that he had no idea why I was there and that he felt it was a waste of funds. That same staff person emailed me after I completed my A.I.R. and said, "thank you for all that you've done for our department." That made me feel like I'd accomplished something.

It's often said that half the battle is showing up. But, the other half is delivering. Sometimes, opportunity is the Mother of Invention.

Given that I had a very short period of time to make an impact, I chose my battles and went with what I felt would have the most impact and what would be the most fun. In such circumstances, you should never underestimate the power of fun. Exuding passion, excitement and a sincere interest is paramount. It's all attitude but most artists aren't going to project those impressions unless the right set of circumstances exists; support, respect, etc.. That holds true in any corporate or government culture.

One of the chief elements of the CCAIR was "support." Across the board, the staff was supportive of my involvement, suggestions and directions. It's rare, unfortunately. Usually, the staff directs the art opportunity, listens more to the community/political constituency and/or weighs consensus over innovation. We can go beyond a community mural, utility box project or a series of light post banners. Those are all viable but they're also standard and therefore tend to be invisible.

LADOT allowed me to explore options that were basically reacting to their internal discussions; in meetings, in the elevators, in the conference rooms and during lunch.

Other opportunities I have had in the past and present have not been as supportive and the work has been less innovative and unfortunately, less interesting. The support I received at LADOT and DCA was freeing. It in turn made me feel open to ideas and consider unfamiliar directions. This a key management and culture building philosophy that resulted in the amount of work I produced, how much time I put in the project and perhaps why we received so much media attention. A healthy, respectful and open environment results in a workforce that will not only have ownership to the work but will respond positively by going above and beyond the expectations of all involved. If all these things are achieved, all involved will also broadcast the work in the future via conversation, conference presentations and other public presentations thereby expanding the work to a broader constituency. Everyone works more because the environment is respectful, clear and concise. They can feel that there's innovation at work and not something mediocre. In my twenty-seven years in government, it was only the second time I experienced this type of team environment.

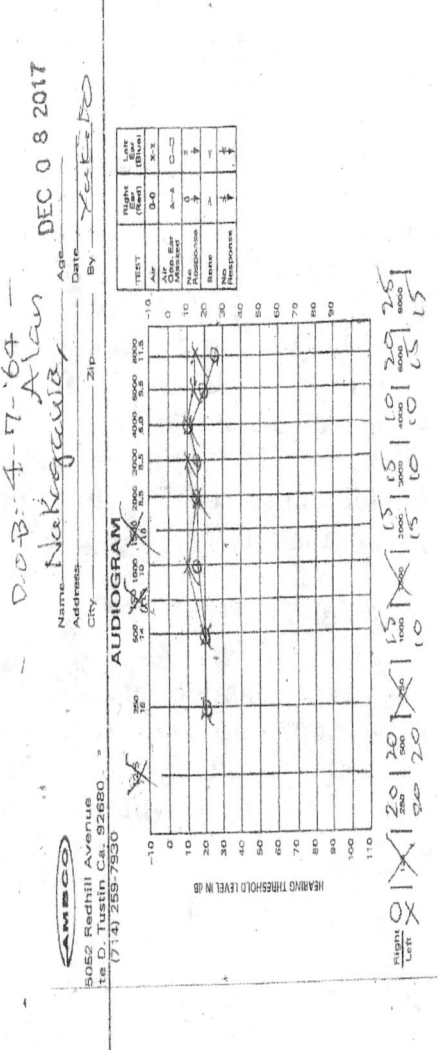

D.O.B: 4-7-'64
Alan

DEC 0 8 2017

Name: Nakagawa
Address:
City: Zip:

Age:
Date:
By: Yoshi FO

| AMBCO |

5052 Redhill Avenue
te D, Tustin Ca. 92680
(714) 259-7930

AUDIOGRAM

HEARING THRESHOLD LEVEL IN dB

TEST	Right Ear (Red)	Left Ear (Blue)
Air	O—O	X—X
Air Otto. Ear Masked	Δ—Δ	□—□
No Response	Ø	❖
Bone	Λ	Υ
No Response	↑	↓

Ronald Shigematsu, M.D.
Sumi Kawaratani, M.D.
420 East Third Street, Suite 705
Los Angeles, CA 90013

MENTAL LOOPS

I was about five (1969-70). I stood in the play-ground. It was a blue sky day in L.A.. We were kindergarteners in Mrs. Brown's class at Wilton Place Elementary School.

By myself for the moment, I kept looking up at the sky because I was playing with the multitude of frequencies I was hearing. This was the moment I realized it was not from outside but from inside my body. I had heard these before, especially right before falling asleep at night or during nap time but at that moment, on the playground, and for the first time, I realized they were actually inside me and not only that but that I could in fact control which pitch was louder, playing it, in matter of speaking, like an organ. There were four to five frequencies or pitches, high and low, not much in between.

The late Oliver Sacks writes about this ability in his book *Musicophilia*. Apparently, we are the only animals who have this ability to focus on a certain sound within a cluster of sounds at will, much like how we can visually zero in on an object or a person in a crowded room. Dogs can do it with their scent, evidently but it's not clear if it's will.

As I am typing this (6:05 AM, 12-27-17) I hear them. It's a quiet morning and there's no music or radio on yet. There's a low sort of rumble that's at center, if you will, as if it were coming out of my forehead. The higher pitches are also constant but don't rumble, rather they are sustained and coming out of the ear or from the sides of my skull. Right now, there are three distinct pitches.

As the day moves on and I get busy, listening to music or the radio, the rest of the folks in the house will start to move around and turn appliances on, and the outside world will begin to move, masking the pitches in my head, becoming unnoticeable.

There was a very brief time in my life that I could also see a kind of color swatch or wave-like movement in connection somehow to sound and objects. It wasn't an aura per se but a kind of after movement. It was during a three-year span in college when I was a vegetarian and then a bit afterwards. Once I began to eat meat again, this ability slowly evaporated. I also recall that some of the colors, I could not describe. They did not exist in the real world.

I also had this ongoing obsession with "3" and corners.

Anything that came in three or the number three was suspect. I would equate it with a kind of premonition and often something negative. My biggest example is in High School, I was traveling with the school hand bell choir (that's another story) and on a meal-stop at a cafe off the highway, we ordered food. I was given my tray and an order number, one of those small bent one-piece plastic number signs, and it was "3." It seemed to stare at me and grow large. I distinctly remember it getting big, almost saying like, "here it comes." Within minutes, John Lennon was murdered. Today, I can see this as a mere coincidence but at that moment, it seemed really connected.

I also used to see what I can only call *ghosts*. There were a number of moments, where I think I saw something or something came to visit. Today, I know there are certain gases emanating out of the earth that can cause one to hallucinate or that there are natural phenomena our brains are quick to personify but back then, I seriously considered the existence of a spirit world. So much so, that I created a system called the *Ladder Theory*.

The Ladder Theory used the system of dimensions much like what is taught in basic drawing. The 2-D of shadows, for instance is manifested by light and dark created by objects in 3-D. 3-D sees the 2-D. Can 2-D see 3-D? Can 4-D see us? The Ladder Theory proposes dismantling the hierarchical system of dimensions. If the dimensions are like steps or rungs on a ladder, let's take them off their place on the ladder, a vertical plane, and suspended or float them in space so as to lose the verticality and numbering system; 1-D, 2-D, 3-D etc.. So as they float in space, they may periodically bump into each other, attach themselves or overlap, or never connect to each other. Sometimes the connections are ongoing/constant, as in shadows and sometimes they are occasional, periodic and/or momentary, as in seeing ghosts. In this theory, there are infinite amounts of steps or dimensions.

Corners: another obsession. I would imagine that every corner, where a plane meets a plane, was shooting out a line. Where the corners connect, a line is generated. I imagined that these lines could become solid, which would most likely result in the death of every living thing on the planet. It was a physics concept with a rather dark outcome. It was my fatalist-geometry theory.

Audio Recording: a pivotal encounter took place one evening while I was helping at my family's restaurant on Olympic Blvd. I must have been around thirteen or fourteen. My aunt's co-worker, Cecilia Tapscott, brought her husband to our Japanese restaurant on Olympic Blvd and Norton Avenue. Horace Tapscott was a renowned pianist and composer and the founder of the Pan Afrikan Peoples Arkestra. He detested the term Jazz. Cecilia had prepped Horace that I was studying Bebop and Swing drums. I suspect my parents were prepped that he was coming and that's why they let me sit with Horace and Cecilia, instead of busing the tables and washing the dishes. The two times this happened were like life lessons for me. I learned so much about the ethnic history of African Americans and American Classic Music (which is what Horace called Jazz). Horace introduced me to Langston Hughes' writings and the importance of African drumming. A couple of years later, in high school, he would invite me to a recording session of the Pan Afrikan Peoples Arkestra. I agreed to go but honestly, I had no clue what a recording session was. My Aunt drove me there and we walked through the doors of the Sunset-Gower Recording Studio, a legendary place in Hollywood. I would spend the next hour or so sitting quietly in front of the mixing counsel in the sound room watching Horace discuss his composition measure by measure on the sprawled-out sheet music with the producer and engineer while fifteen or so musicians waited patiently on the other side of the double pane window. I didn't say anything and no one spoke to me. I soaked it in like a dry sponge to water and as my Aunt drove me home I lit up like a bonfire, *AHA! that's how the music I listen to on the record gets recorded.* It had never really occurred to me that there was a process to recording at that scale. Within a couple of years, I would purchase my first multi-track recorder, a TEAC 3340S reel to reel four-track with remote, starting my obsession with audio recording.

In college, I learned about the cochlea and that changed everything. Here was a shell-like object inside us, a great symbolic shape. It's how we hear. Having been born and raised near the ocean, the connection of this shape seemed meaningful. Who doesn't love to put a seashell next to their ear (which is less about hearing what's inside the shell than it is actually reinforcing what is being heard in your ear) and it brought me closer to understanding my tinnitus.

At Otis Art Institute (1982-86) we had a science

teacher named Nick Warren. His courses were geared toward artists. I loved those classes. From the study of sound waves via Newton to color frequencies via Goethe and there was Wucius Wong' and Josef Albers studies as well. Nick showed us the similarities between soundwaves and light waves. For the first time, I had a vocabulary to explain my attraction to recording. I was especially inspired by the work of Michael Brewster (who I would later be introduced to via Thinh Nguyen during the Ear Meal Webcast productions, 2010's), who had created sound installations that utilized the physical characteristics of frequencies and interiors.

In graduate school (UC Irvine, 1986-88), I was able to meet an audiologist for the first time at the UC Irvine Medical Center. She gave me a brief introduction to hearing and our hearing apparatus. It was an experience I have never forgotten and it inspired a series of art work at the time.

In 2008, I experienced my first sound bath at the Integratron in Joshua Tree, CA. That inspired all of the vibratory sound work I've been presenting since, often utilizing my Sound Beds, large aluminum beds with speakers in them. During this period, I was introduced to the work of Royal Rife, a 1930's scientist who allegedly created a machine that could generate frequencies through a reverse x-ray technology. He had figured out the anti-soundwaves of the frequencies of pathogens and documented the elimination of certain cancer-causing cells in patients. I discovered these frequency clusters online and began to use them as a micro-tonal vocabulary for my music/sound work.

I curated the weekly webcast Ear Meal Webcast via LA ArtStream. Ear Meal Webcast documented the L.A. sound art and experimental music community. This afforded me a kind of Masters course in experimental sound creation, much of which inspired my work. In addition to these influences, I became a member of the Southern California Soundscape Ensemble, a field recording orchestra, which prompted me to use field recordings in my own work and this led me to the three-point recordings of interiors I have been working on since.

What all this led to, in my mind, was the residency at the Smithsonian Museum of American History, where I researched the history of the hearing aid and the House Ear institute where I was introduced to the details of the cochlea and organ of corti.

Our hearing mechanism processes airborne sound waves and translates them into electrons, the language of the brain. It's like our voices are translated into electrical current when we speak into a microphone. This revelation was incredible to me and has been an inspiration for me these past few years.

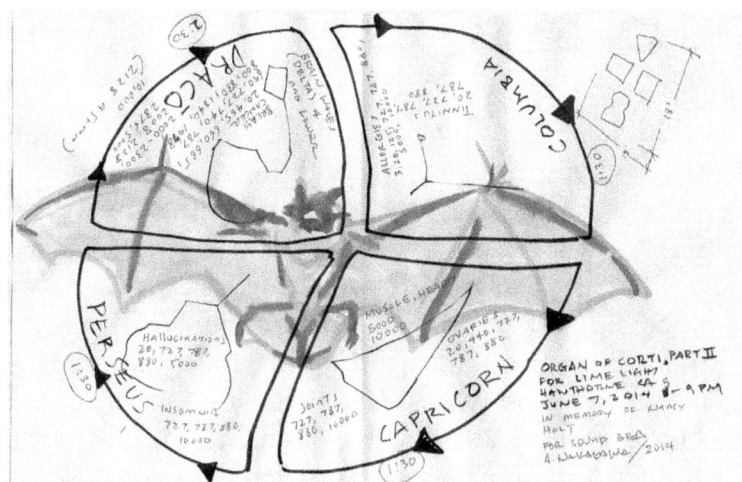

Organ of Corti Part II Sound Map, Cordary Arts, 2014

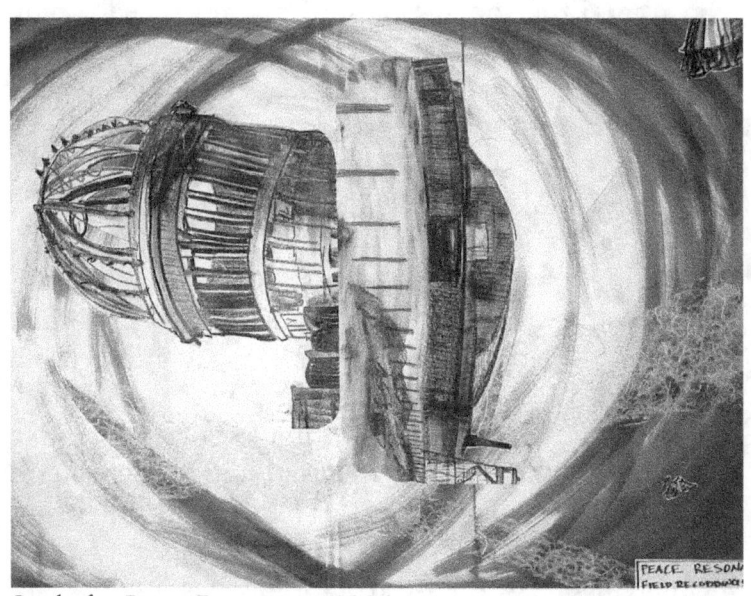

Study for Peace Resonance, 2016

BONES

In the Japanese American community, it's common to enroll your kids in Saturday Japanese School, especially if your parents are from Japan, as were my parents. The school I went to was close to our home in what is now Koreatown. Looking back, it was a colorful experience but at the time it was mostly about play and had little to do with studying Japanese, which is why I didn't last very long at that school. One day, during one of the breaks, one of the students in our class, who was much older, for some reason, decided to take me for a ride on his bicycle. I don't remember exactly why. The school was off Olympic Blvd in an area where there are small hills. So, I'm sitting on his rack of his ten speed, going uphill and I'm like seven years old and I slip and my left arm gets caught in the spokes of his back wheel. I remember several things about this:

1) All the spokes of the back wheel were busted and dangling off the rim
2) Walking back to the school, my left arm had the sensation of a taught rubber band that was winding tight and then loosening the other way and around and then back, around and then back.
3) Our family Doctor never forgot about how brave I was throughout the entire visit up until he brought out a needle, then I guess I lost it and balled out crying.
4) Having a cast on my arm for months was my first time experiencing my healing body.

5) Not being able to play or be active led to stress eating. This period was the start of my weight problem.

* * *

The first time I met my Grandmother, my Father's Mother, I was around seven or eight. She came from Japan to visit us. We would remain close till she passed away much later in life. One day, she was at the family house making a large pot of miso soup in the kitchen and like the clueless kid I was, I ran into the kitchen, into her and the entire pot of boiling soup washed onto me. The pain was numbing. The scream was piercing. My instinct kicked in and I ran into the backyard and jumped into the pool we had erected for the summer.

I spent about nine months in bed with a cast on my upper body. I know my Grandmother felt guilty about this till the day she died but oddly, I think this bonded us for life. Whenever my family talks about this episode, they always say how they tried to tell my Grandmother it wasn't her fault but we all knew how she really felt.

Nine months is a long time to lay on the couch. I watched a lot of television and ate a lot of junk food and this put my weight problem into hyper-drive. Pictures of me after this period of my life are unbelievable. Awful fashion sense and the oddly long hair aside, my self-esteem took a nosedive. That weight problem and junk food eating habit would just continue till the age of thirteen.

* * *

One afternoon, during recess at Wilton Place Elementary School, my friends and I were playing on a pile of poles that were laying at the end of the playground. These poles were the various poles that were used for the basketball hoops, volleyball nets, etc. So on one end was the concrete footing that held them into the ground. I am not sure why they were dug up and laying in a pile but for us it was a new playground equipment. In retrospect, it's amazing that no one told us not to play on that pile. I had climbed on this heap with some others and all of a sudden, one of the poles swung and the footing smacked me in my eye.

I managed to get off the pile and walk towards the nurse's office. I think one of the teachers escorted me there. The distance between the pile of poles and the nurse's office was the playground. They were on opposite sides. I remember walking and feeling like I was facing straight ahead of me but my right eye kept looking at the floor of the playground. I think what happened is that the force of the pole and footing had wacked my eye off in the socket temporarily. I don't remember what the treatment in the nurse's office was but at some point, I was back in class.

* * *

In college, Otis Art Institute, I was very much into

multi-media performance art. For one class, I had created a movement and film work for a hallway. In order to make the hallway dark enough for the projection, I had to install a curtain in the hallway. I turned off the lights and started hanging the curtain. In retrospect, I should have hung the curtain and then turned off the lights. When I finished hanging the curtain, I jumped off the step ladder and landed on a roll of duct tape. It was painful but I had to do the performance because our class was on its way. So, I finished the performance and went to the hospital because, as it turned out, I had broken my foot. Doing the movements in the hallway performance with a broken metatarsal turned out to be effective because the Butoh-inspired work seemed to be enhanced by the navigation of pain and balance I was experiencing in that dark hallway.

* *

The last thing I wanted to mention was in every case, my doctors allowed me to keep the xrays. I have a selection of xrays that document these mishaps in my life and it's part of my personal photo album.

ORAL HISTORY

On the rare occasion I've been asked to present my work to students, I always speak about the importance oral history technique has been for my art making process.

The ability and craft of listening is the key. In my on-going quest to make work that resonance with those I work with, I seek for some sense of honesty or truth.

The capacity to listen, the craft of listening and allowing yourself to listen is almost the antithesis of how we as artists are trained. To have mindful clarity, awareness of intention and the relationship to history is what the art critique format in school taught me but what it didn't teach me was to listen. I heard but I didn't listen because listening takes insight, which I didn't have much of at the age of seventeen and the art critique format was often short; the professor had to engage with a dozen or more projects in two hours or so.

The better format for dialogue and therefore a better chance for listening is the studio visit. That's usually a one on one scenario and hopefully an allocation of several hours. It may also include a meal and beverages which always helps any situation where there might be some form of tension or expectation.

When I was curating Ear Meal Webcast, I would

always end the booking of an artist with, "What's your favorite beverage?" We didn't have a budget other than our own bank accounts so we never paid the artists. I thought the least we could do is offer them a drink. In the six years we ran Ear Meal Webcast, I feel I had a secondary function as a bartender. There was a joy in presenting the drink to the artist once they were settled in the studio, which was my garage. Often, they would forget I had asked the question during the scheduling and would be very pleased to have their favorite drink handed to them or made available. It shows that you care and you should. They are taking the time to meet with and help you with your objective. Artists should be made to feel welcomed and comfortable.

When I worked for the public art program for the LA Metro, my first decade there was primarily working with community members to gather cultural data to present to the design team of the communities future rail station. I learned early on that when I walked into the room of community members, I was wearing the metaphoric badge of government. In the course of introducing myself and the project, I would often ask, since I was going to spend several months, if not years in their community, where good places to eat were. Food is a cultural verb that most people attach local pride and identity to. I know I do. An even deeper dig is if you begin to discuss what they love to cook or even what were some of their favorite food dishes growing up. This opens the door to talking about family, which I always love to talk about.

Government is a monolith, at least, from afar. Get closer to that monolith and you begin to see the porous make-up of the structure. Essentially, government is people. The bigger the government, the more people it consists of. It's sort of like a family. The more immediate members, the more diverse the relationships, roles and expectations are. Some family members you love and some you don't look forward to seeing at the holiday party.

When I was co-producing Ear Meal, my co-worker Zipporah Lax-Yamamoto was completing her Doctoral at the University of California Los Angeles. She asked if I was interviewing the artists participating in the show and I said I hadn't considered that. She felt that the opportunity of them coming over my house and performing live in my garage was good but the curation was interesting enough for it to eventually have academic worthiness and oral histories of these artists would be valuable. I don't recall if I even knew what an oral history was at the time but Z gave me an email she had received from Teresa Barnett, the Director of the UCLA Oral History Department. Teresa ran oral history workshops open to the public and I signed up.

Much of what the oral history technique consists of, I had already been incorporating in my art making practice with Collage Ensemble and my day-gig at Metro, in terms of breaking the ice, setting parameters and asking the right questions but letting people speak. What was so amazing to learn was the connecting of the dots between group empowerment, sound engineering and the function/apparatus of hearing.

It was at Teresa Barnett's workshops where I began to build the importance of all of these things as part of my art practice and what could be the process and the outcome through gathering stories and insight. I guess I had separated these processes in my mind but all of a sudden it made sense to see them as all part of a whole. For instance, let's take the idea of fidelity. In audio, it's the caliber of clarity and dynamics or resolution but more importantly it's the richness of the experience of listening to music/audio.

If I go to an art party, I might be introduced to someone for the first time. You can usually figure out how good someone's communications skills are in about three minutes;

*Do they talk about themselves mostly?
*Do they ask you questions? If they do, do they let you elaborate or do they turn the conversation back to them?
*Are they scanning the room while they're talking to you?
*Do you feel engaged in a conversation? What are the elements of feeling engaged?
*While they are speaking, are you really listening or are you thinking about how you want to reply or add to the conversation. If you're doing the later, you aren't really listening to them.

*In oral history, you should be doing little or no talking. If this doesn't appeal to you, maybe you should consider either figuring out how you can train yourself to not speak so much or not engage in oral history? Beware being the interviewer who does most of the talking during a session.

Every occasion of social interaction can be a wonderful opportunity to practice the oral history technique and at the same time make you a better listener. I've heard the adjective "selfless" when someone describes some of my art practice. I don't see it that way at all. When I was at Metro, I got to help build the Docent program. We needed a group to help free up the staff from giving tours of the stations, a request that would come in like rainfall especially around the opening of a new leg of the alignment. This amazing group of individuals collectively became the spokespersons of our art program and in many ways the agency. What attracted them to volunteering for such an assignment? Generally speaking, it was the access to information. i.e. access to the artists, their methodology, details to the design/fabrication/installation process and access to way more information than most Metro staff had. Access to information is access to power. The more you listen, the more unique data becomes available to you and in the case of an oral history, we dig to get access to information currently unavailable. Our job as oral historians is to shut up and listen. It's not an easy thing to do, especially if you get excited about the subject matter. If your participant says something you want to interject your personal connection with, jot it down and bring it up later. If you're effective, you'll open up a stream, a river or the flood gates to memory and history. Don't be a dam.

ORAL HISTORY II

As I've mentioned elsewhere in this book, I was the first grandchild on my Mother's side so I always had fun looking after my cousins at family functions. One of my fondest memories is walking down the street with one of my cousins and having a conversation. At the time, he was around five years old and I was a teenager. Even though we didn't see each other regularly, he was so open to talking with me. I asked questions and he described his life and thoughts. I love that memory so much. I enjoyed listening to him and his thinking process. He was so observant and articulate as such an young age.

When I was in Japan, I once saw on television, an interview of Tetsuko Kuroyanagi. (Which would be the Japan's equivalent to our Barbara Walters.) At the time, I didn't know who she was. What struck me was when she spoke about her early education. She must have been very young but it was about the time she interviewed for Tomoe Elementary School. She said up to that moment, she was known to be a quiet child or maybe the culture was that kids weren't supposed to talk like they are encouraged today. There's that old saying, children should be seen but not heard. The headmaster of Tomoe sat down with her and started asking questions. Kuroyanagi or Totto-chan as she is known started to answer his questions. She said, it might have been the first time an adult wanted to know her opinion. She said they talked for over an hour. Here's this high-level authority, sitting down with her one-on-one and actively listening to her. She said she couldn't believe it but it opened the flood gates of thoughts she had up to that moment in her young life.

When I began to study Oral History at the University of California Los Angeles, and began to utilize it in my art practice, I was introduced to the idea of permission. We need permission to tell our stories. Whether it's permission from the headmaster of the school or even yourself, getting permission isn't so much about being granted but rather entering a safe zone where you can disclose personal and often introspective thoughts to another person and in many cases to the world. In this age of soundbites and text messaging, the in-depth forum of Oral History technique is a navigation of sorts to comprehensive dialogue encouraged by active listening.

Oral History technique is a chance to listen to someone's intricacies and dig deeper than an interview or a conversation. When I'm conducting an oral history, I am asking initial questions but I'm trying to do less talking and more listening. I am trying to let the person guide me to information. There's the saying, leave no stone unturned. It's not necessarily that. You often don't have an infinite amount of time for sessions and most people get tired after an hour or so. However, a person who feels comfortable to disclose will often have an idea, however vague, of what's important and what's not. Often, they glance over details that may seem trivial to them but are in fact doorways to tributaries of information. I often say, you wanna leave an oral history session with someone remarking things like, "wow, I never told anyone about that before," "I never realized that had such an impact on me," or maybe days or weeks later, "I'm still thinking about our oral history session, that really resonated with me."

If at all possible, a second session may be beneficial. If you built a sanctuary of comfort at the first session, the second session should be able to dig even deeper to more details and uncharted fields of history.

I highly recommend one-on-one sessions. Try to avoid more than one person at all costs. The moment there's a third person or more, you decrease the opportunity of candid thoughts and sharing. Otherwise, you have to manage two stories or more and they have to manage the sharing and thinking between them. Always design toward the win-win scenario.

If there's information online, books, articles, home-pages about the person, study them as much as possible beforehand. I will say that I am more interested in conducting an oral history session with someone who wouldn't have that much information about themselves online. I once interviewed someone who was trending online at the time and found that every reply felt like it was written or it was a version he had decided to use having answered the questions so many times before. It takes more time to warm down those canned answers and get to new territory with someone who is used to being interviewed or asked in the spotlight. On the other hand, if there's so much information available on someone, maybe a strategy would be to talk about something they have never talked about in public. I have often used that as a question i.e. is there someone who influenced you early on who you have never spoken about?

Not everyone is equipped to do oral histories. You have to have the ability to not talk about yourself. You may think that you have an experience just like or that relates to what they are talking about but the oral history is not about you. If the session ends and you haven't disclosed anything about yourself, that's very successful. I am totally aware that it's difficult to do. I certainly have been guilty of going on diatribes about my experiences during a session but what it often does is break the thought process of the person you are interviewing not to mention a lot more editing out later on.

There are people who need to turn conversations around so it's always about themselves. They interject that they have an experience that's just like yours. As an oral historian, it's your job to be the opposite of such a person. Is it a selfless task? Not necessarily but you do need to be observant, be able to understand cues, body language, hidden content and context. It's hard to do all that while you're also trying to think about how to add your story into the session. If you are doing that then most likely you aren't listening as well.

At this point, I've conducted over six hundred oral history sessions. This may seem like a lot but compared to veteran oral historians in the field, it's a tiny amount. I am still surprised at what people disclose and what pieces of their lives they are willing to uncover. It's a remarkable privilege to do oral histories of people. You capture voice both figuratively and literally. I'll never forget the workshops at UCLA's Oral History Program. Teresa Barnett would lead these classes on how to do oral histories but she would sort of use the technique of oral histories to engage us in the class. Of course, we probably didn't realize it at the time. The ability to orchestrate engagement is key to oral history and it's not always the same. When I was studying jazz drumming, the term "play the room" was often something my teacher, Hugh Allison, would talk about. It means that although you're playing what you're playing, listen to how your drums sound in that room, how the music sounds in the room and most importantly, how the audience is reacting to the music. How does reading the room relate to oral history? The "room" is not only the space between the person and you but also the rooms of their history and stories. You are in a partnership with the person, navigating their rooms of history, secrets and forgotten moments.

MY ATTEMPT TO WRITE ABOUT:

"DREAMERS; Cornell told me that birdhouses are dreamcatchers/ for Shizue Yamashiro"
on my artist website:
I presented this in January-February 2018 at Visitors Welcome Center in Koreatown, LA CA. The opening artist reception was January 20, 2018.

dreamers; cornell said birdhouses are dreamcatchers/ for shizue yamashiro

It was inspired by Joseph Cornell's boxes and the passing of my first art teacher, Shizue Yamashiro.

It was a semi-symmetrical bed, sound tunnel, dream station, inverted Cornell shadow box, costume and featured my perfume, "Cornell."

Thank you to Visitor Welcome Center, ArtPlace and the Institute of Art and Olfaction.

thoughts (12-09-17 @ 4:00 AM);

I think I'm ready to write about this piece.

Let's start in the beginning. (I shouldn't make any apologies)

It was the end of the 2016-17 exhibition season for Visitors Welcome Center and I asked David Bell the

Gallery Director and artist Iris Yirei Hu if it would be of interest for me to perform a private sound work in the empty gallery space, in celebration of a great season, I had an interest to fill the rooms with sound and to offer my version of a kind of cleansing or closure. After a few exchanges and thoughts, we scheduled an evening (08-04-17).

I prepared a map of the piece and practiced it twice in my studio with my effect pedals, loopers and oscillators. The piece was simple, in that, I wanted to project soundwaves into the empty rooms and bathe the walls with sound.

Everyone helped get the equipment up the stairs. Setting up was simple and there I was with David, Iris and laub.

We turned the lights out so that the street lights came through the glass windows, a grid that changed every time cars passed below. It was an amazing found animation. You could really see the difference between the older and newer glass; old hand created glass (textured) and newer machine created glass (very smooth).

My sound work was no more than 23 minutes and I titled it *Frequency Response VWC 080417*.

I brought my Fender Princeton Reverb, a vintage guitar tube amplifier. I placed it in the northeast corner of the east room with the 10" speaker facing the wall. I set the volume loud enough to get a dynamic range but not too loud as to drown out the outside ambience.

The performance and the discussion afterwards and really the soaking in of the moment, experience and company, was really incredibly moving to me. It was something I wanted to do but had no perception of what its meaning was until, of course, I got back home.

A long story shortened, David generously offered a two-person show in November which later became a solo show in January 2018. That was not my intention but obviously as a fan of the gallery, I was dumfounded and hyper-grateful.

On August 8, 2017, I was in Chicago for a two-hour meeting for ArtPlace, of which I was a panelist. I extended my stay originally to spend time with my then girlfriend but we had ended the relationship in the interim and I was faced with several unplanned extra days in Chicago. Having been offered a show at VWC, I had this idea of seeing the Joseph Cornells at the Chicago Art Institute. They have the largest collection of Cornells. I had seen some of them in 2004 but it was a brief viewing. At that time, as I recall, there was remodeling being done at the museum and the bulk of the collection was not on view. So, 13 years later, this chance to really spend time with them was exciting and timely.

I ended up drawing them, studying them and sort of letting them penetrate my mind's eye. I stood in front of them for two and a half days drawing them. Taking pictures with my phone, I would make watercolors of them in my hotel room at night, returning to the gallery during the day.

When I draw, if all is going well, I get into a zone. I think this is very common for artists. I get to a place where I am focusing on a kind of relationship between what I am seeing and what I am drawing with the periodic brain conversation of drafting. It's mostly intuitive and second nature, like dreaming.

The way it works in the museum is you can't drink in the gallery. You have to go outside the museum or downstairs to their cafe. However, the guard did let me drink once out of my water bottle the first day. Typically, I am brain numb and a bit dehydrated by the time I pull myself away to rest from drawing. That one time, it was the first day so I walked out to the gallery where there's a bench next to the window overlooking a park and I sat, faced the outside and drank my water. The guard, I suspect knowing that I had been drawing for several hours or so, I don't remember the duration, walked over and said no one is allowed to drink inside the gallery but she'll give me a pass this one time.

I loved drawing the boxes. They are in a darkened hall with 23 boxes in a large glass display. The hall was dimly lit and the boxes are dimly lit with soft spotlights. I started on one end and just went one column of boxes at a time over two and a half days.

Occasionally, people would wander through, no one really spent time looking at the boxes. Maybe three times during the course of this exercise, a group of school kids with sketch pads would join me in drawing the boxes. I loved that very much but as quickly as they arrived, they would leave. I wished I could have seen their drawings but I was too focused on what I was doing.

During the three days, there were unsuspected moments;

1. Due to Museum policy I couldn't use the pens I brought and needed to purchase pencils (luckily there was a Blick Art Store nearby)

2. A friend, who I studied with in Osaka, saw my posts, and texted he and his family happened to be in Chicago too. I got to meet his wife and daughter for the first time

3. One of the days, I came early so I sat in this tree sanctuary to the side of the museum. As I walked toward a bench that wasn't occupied, a grasshopper hovered past me. It turns out a dragon fly was transporting it. I sat down and started to draw. At one point I looked up from my sketch pad and the and grasshopper was on floor right in front of me. I waited to see if the dragon fly was going to return but it never did.

The cafe latte downstairs in the museum was wonderful, which I enjoyed the last day but by and large I was in that dark hall, drawing the boxes, alone in silence. Halfway through, I thought that I wasn't going to finish. There were just too many and the choreography of drawing and the growing need to spend more time with each box was burning away my limited time. In other words, as my eye adjusted, my brain and eye coming to terms of what I was seeing and drawing, I began to feel, each time, like I could feel Cornell making the box; deciding, deliberate gestures and symbolic and/or metaphoric decision-making systems. There's way more there than meets the eye. You could really sense a kind of pre-meditation; scholarly, personal aesthetic pushing intuition and craft.

It's not like I could sense Cornell in the room as much as his processes' patina or a kind of process residue.

It probably comes down to what attracts me to his work from the start; this portal to the dream state. This deep connection to history and the inherent connectivity of events, facts and information. That which we call science, history, psychology, engineering, spirituality, literature and art. They are like postcards from a parallel universe. They are music without sound.

In the book *N.P.* or was it *Lizard*?, by Banana Yoshimoto, there's a character that builds objects. He's a sculptor, an artist and the story is from the point of view of his girlfriend who brokers the selling of these objects. There's something about the form, weight, texture, and vibration, of these objects, that sits well in each of its recipient's hands. Those lucky enough to purchase one find them healing and transformative. There's a vetting process where they meet prospective buyers. If he doesn't like them or gets a bad vibe, he won't make one for them. It's a point of contention between the couple primarily regarding economics; selling a product vs the destiny of an object.

In one of the articles I read about Cornell, he was reluctant to sell his work. He actually purposely did not live in NY. He was sort of a recluse in comparison to his contemporaries. In fact, I read one narrative by a dealer who had to trick Cornell into selling him his work. There's also stories of artist Yayoi Kusama spending time with the elder Cornell and brokering work for a dealer.

This ability or mode to create art that doesn't quite work well within a capitalist model is something I am attracted to or rather a place I always find myself. I think this is partially why I worked in government for so long. This route for a steady vocation that would allow me to negotiate time to cultivate my aesthetic is something or a conclusion or a path that I arrived at early on while I was studying at Otis. I accepted the fact that I would most likely never fit in the gallery system nor would I be able to create solo work until about my late 40's early 50's. I felt that I needed to live a life before I could truly make anything I felt had sufficient content. It's a thought that I would remember throughout my adulthood. It's been a point of pain and a point of solace. Most importantly, I allowed myself time to grow before I became a solo artist, although twenty-five years of collaborations was essential for me.

Starting in 2008, my "solo" path as an artist began to show some promise. Starting with the invitation to participate in Scratch produced by SASSAS and also the invitation to create a sound component for the opening of BCAM at LACMA, I gradually would end my collaborative work and with a lion's share of opportunities and awards, I found myself, nine years later with a body of work that expressed my experiences, connections and vocabulary, that had been incubating all those years.

(ok, I'm getting sleepy again. it's 5:34 AM)

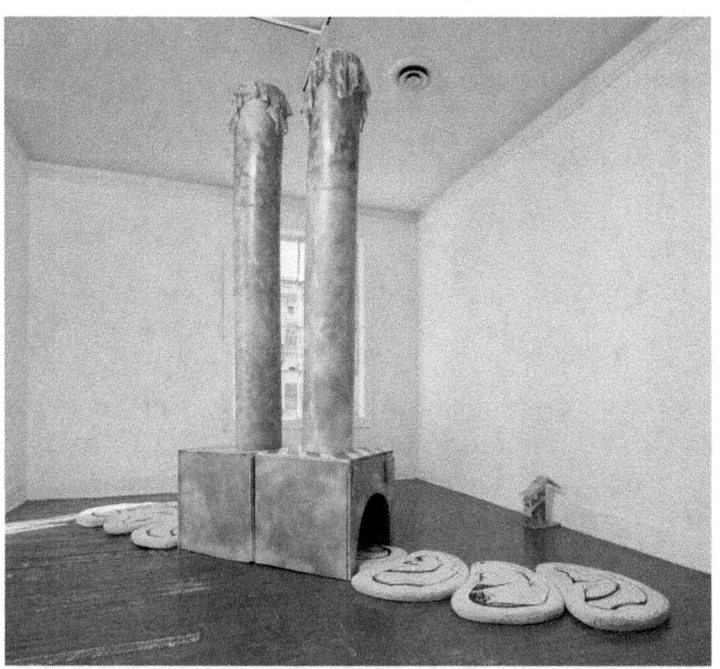

Dreamers; Cornell Said Birdhouses are Dream Catchers/ for Shizue
Yamashiro
Photo by Elon Schoenholz

SAVE 800 TRACTION AVENUE CAMPAIGN

December 9, 2017, 10:32 AM;
I was asked to give a public comment at the City of Los Angeles Cultural Heritage Commission in support of 800 Traction Avenue's Tenants; artists who had lived there for decades and represent the original artist population of the Arts District. They had received eviction notices to make way for a high-end apartment complex with high-end retail at the street level. This final enclave of artist studios in the Arts District had gained considerable momentum and I was asked to speak about my history with the building. I read the following statement:

> Thank you (Commissioners) for letting me speak today
>
> My name is Alan Nakagawa
>
> My parents immigrated from Hiroshima in 1957. I was born and raised in L.A. As a child, I had a knack for drawing, so at age 9, I was enrolled in art classes near L.A. High, taught by Tokyo artist Shizue Yamashiro.
>
> This teacher would talk about a famous Japanese artist who taught at the local art college, Otis Art Institute. "Maybe I should go

there for college", she would say.

A decade later, I made it into Otis and it was during that time that I was invited on several occasions to 800 Traction Ave, to Mike Kanemitsu and Nancy Uyemura's studio. Mike was the Japanese American artist my art teacher kept talking about.

Mike would have students over to talk about art history and we would share meals. That circle of young talent included Gajin Fujita, who is now in LACMA's permanent collection and Kris Kuramitsu who is the director of the art gallery the Mistake Room, part of the Getty's current Pacific Standard Time.

Art history is dominated by white male artists, so it made a difference to have a community of professional artists who were also Asian and Asian American.

35 years later, I am still a practicing artist. I am a recipient of the City of L.A.'s Artist Fellowship or COLA and a California Community Foundation Mid-Career Artist Fellowship.

Last year, I was selected as the City's first Creative Catalyst Artist in Resident and worked with the Department of Transportation for one year.

This position afforded me the privilege of representing Los Angeles nationally on panels for the NEA, Transportation for America, the Smithsonian Museum of American History and ArtPlace.

I am currently the artist for Great Streets, through the Mayor's office, where I am collaborating with eight LA neighborhoods on improving various urban infrastructures.

The time I spent at 800 Traction empowered me and I am not the only one. There are a number of us who are making a difference in the community, who benefited from this informal nexus.

Thank you.

I have no idea if what I said resonated with anyone but it was awesome to be amongst some amazing and historically important artists and historians, each giving our side of the importance of the cause and the significance of the 800 Traction Ave Artist Studio. Well, the commission ended up passing the developers proposal anyway, which means we lost that battle.

I've been re-visiting, for over a year now, the connection I have with the Japanese American art community and specifically my first art teacher, as I mention in my comment, Shizue Yamashiro, or as I would always call her, "Sensei": Japanese for *teacher* or *professor*.

On February 6, 2016, Sensei Yamashiro passed away. I was her student from 1970 to 1981 and she was instrumental in giving me the tools to make it into Otis and everything that followed. I believe that walking into Otis in 1982, with a certain level of drawing and painting skills, allowed me to be open to the sound, collaborative and performative art genres I was introduced to there. Entering Otis, I was equipped to saturate myself with all of this new genre information my teachers were eager to share.

Once I wasn't attending Sensei's school, I lost touch with her, unfortunately. Decades later I did see her and her husband, writer Mas Yamashiro, at the Japanese American Cultural and Community Center. Well, she did remember me but I got the distinct feeling I was one of hundreds of kids who took classes from her so although it was great to see them there was no connection per se. But, I never forgot her influence and I've tried to acknowledge her whenever I had the chance. Her passing away really hit me so this piece is dedicated to her; her immigration story to the US and her generous guidance into the visual arts is what set the tone for this work.

NOTE: When I arrived in the crowded Cultural Heritage Commission meeting at City Hall, David Monkawa, Veteran Community Leader and Artist, signaled that there was a seat in the back. I walked over and sat down but before I did he grabbed me by the arm and whispered in my ear that in back of me are the Developers who are working for Suisse Bank, the new owners of 800 Traction Avenue.

During one of the community comments, a resident was expressing how she felt it was immoral for these foreign companies to come into her neighborhood and displace the long-time residents who help build the Arts District. It was then I heard one of the three Developers in back of me say, "Welcome to America," and then the three of them laughed.

DECEMBER 13, 2017

Wow, still reading?

Tonight, I finally finished reading bell hooks' book, *Belonging*. It's the first book of hooks I've ever read. About a year or so ago, I was walking with Carol Zou along the LA River near the WCCW (she had a residency there). We were talking about the transitional space we both were in. I leaving Metro after 25 years and she beginning her work with the immigrant community in Dallas via Rick Lowe. We spoke about teaching and pedagogy. I'd never taught in a college or university and she suggested I read *Teaching Community; A Pedagogy of Hope*. I bought it and lost the book. I bought it a second time and left it at an REI sale. I then purchased *Belonging; A Culture of Place*. This time I didn't lose it and read it from cover to cover.

It'd been a while since I read a book that affected me so much, so emotional. It's a tapestry of subject matter or more appropriate, a quilt of thoughts and meanings. There is much in the book that echoes my life, especially at this juncture; home, not fitting in the others as an *other*, home coming, parents and grandparents, racism, white supremacy, intellectualism, cultivating the critical mind, etc.

I am a fan of Alvin Lucier's work. This year, my friend went to Documenta and sent me images of his exhibition. In his didactic, Lucier describes himself as a phenomenologist. I appreciate the concept of phenomenology because on one level, that's the aesthetic dialogue I contribute to, in part. However, as a person of color, I can't subjugate myself and my practice to that wholly. By doing so, I would be in the camp that believes we are in a post-racial society and I don't believe that we are anywhere near such a state. It's a conundrum I wrestle with. On one hand, I was trained in a Duchampian dominated art making practice and on the other my personal experience is partially unique due in part to my not being white in the United States. It doesn't help that I am currently reading Martin Heidegger's *Phenomenology of Intuition and Expression*, where he systematically seems to be breaking down self-experience and meaning. I'm only half way through the book but it seems to ignore social politics and class politics. Honestly, it feels like 75% of the time, I have no idea what he's talking about.

These two books are informing my work and specifically *DREAMERS; Cornell told me that birdhouses are dream catchers/ for Shizue Yamashiro.*

Let me end on the perfume. So, the entire work is a dedication to Sensei through this love for Cornell's boxes but it's the perfume, titled *Cornell* that is actually the portrait of Joseph Cornell. It's a multi-referential work. The scent was created at the Institute of Art and Olfaction in Chinatown. I constructed it after my trip to Chicago. I was thinking musty dark attic full of things but with the familiarity of a scholar-angel (this is where the Jonathan Winters reference comes in; Winters' Attic skit. I grew watching a lot of television variety shows and Winters' was one of my favorites, especially this attic segment he often did at the end of the show. An attic set filled with objects and he would randomly pick something up and build an entire character and story around it. It was a testament to his genius). In a sense, I'm idolizing these two white males who represent genius (Cornell and Winters) and inspiration which contrasts what the piece is about; contemporary immigration and the POC experience. Well, most of my mentors are POC and women but there are a few white males and females who are also mentors so I acknowledge that. It's complicated, as it should be.

The perfume represents the ephemeral and the all-encompassing nature of a spirit or other worldly protector/mentor. The work is also a mask because once someone is in it, they are in fact wearing it. The perfume is the invisible element, the pervasive element, the spirit world element, as if a channeling takes place once in the piece. Inside the piece, you are in a birdhouse. Views outside see someone wearing the birdhouse; they are witnessing someone laying, alluding to resting, sleeping and dreaming. It's an utopian state.

Well, I think that's enough. There are a few more points but I'll leave that to another avenue; immigration, wanting for participants to fall asleep and dream, the sound element of the duct while inside, the fact that there are two and ......

A SONG I SANG AT THE END OF A DREAM THIS MORNING BOOK DROP 2018

My soul was raised, by turtles and cranes
They told me not to reach, for riches or fame
Sometimes it feels, this is crumbling sand
Waiting for the pendulum, swing to drier land

My heroes are spirits, that point to the goal
But on my map, less yeses than no's
I know in my heart, all this could change
In the meantime, it's more of the same

(chorus) Where are you now ? Where are you now ?
Where are you now my sweet, sweet love ?
Where are you now ? Where are you now ?
Where are you now my sweet, sweet love ?

Sometimes your lost, but your eyes still glow
Lived no regrets, but now they stand in rows
There's a rage that rings, that we once shared
Days that end, wondering if it's still there
(chorus)

There's no rock won't move
Norms once impossible
Remember what you wished
Start again your unstoppable (2x)

We're all waiting, for someone to lead
Is that the crop, that harvests no seed?
Where the dollar is god, no balance in sight
Where change is the dream, when will it take
flight?

(chorus)

GARDEN ESSAY

Around 2010, we started to see this ridiculous drought in Southern California raise its ugly head. By 2014, our lawns and hillsides were barren, brown and dry. Here in Los Angeles, we saw a lot of government and non-profit initiatives in response. You had to decrease the frequency of watering your lawn or otherwise pay a fine if you got cited. Some neighbors were actually telling on other neighbors if they saw "excessive" watering or disregard to this new ordinance. We started to see artificial turf installed onto City sidewalks. Reduced prices or free rain barrels and compost bins were distributed. My backyard became a dirt lot. It was like a mini-dustbowl; This Land is Your Land!

In 2015, I took a class on drought tolerant landscaping at the Theodore Payne Foundation, a local non-profit dedicated to indigenous and drought tolerant plants. Not too long after that class, I was honored to spend six weeks at the MacDowell Art Colony in Peterborough, New Hampshire. Of course, there was no drought in Peterborough, quite the opposite. It's a lush forest and it rained and thundered all the time. In fact, it inspired my sound sculpture, Mudsling; a twenty-four-foot aluminum sound bed vibrating from an audio loop based on a stereo recording of a thunderstorm that came through MacDowell one afternoon.

There's a remarkable garden surrounding the main

building at MacDowell. One day, the head gardener gave a few of us a tour. It was inspirational and taught me that gardening is a relationship not a conquer. The "rules" are more gray than black-and-white, it helps to have a direction or philosophy or theme. When I got back to LA, I was armed with a new outlook to gardening and started to cultivate my barren backyard.

The garden or my butterfly sanctuary is a lot full of distant life. It is a portal to a different scale of consciousness. I am the caretaker who has little idea or training on how to maintain a garden so most of the time, I'm winging it. I primarily weed, clean, rake, soak and prune.

I show up once a week to this self-assigned part time job. I can't tell you what I planted and I don't know the names of the types of butterflies that show up. I have ID signs in front of all the plants in case guests want to know the name of the plants. My job is to keep it at a certain level of existence.

There are monarch-looking butterflies, yellow butterflies that catch the sunlight well, black with spots of color that are majestic, white ones that seem solemn and starting a couple of weeks ago these tiny butterflies with peacock-like splotches started to show up. These, in particular, are so small and fast that I haven't actually had a good look at them. There are "jumpers" too, which are small and moth-like.

I did purchase a California butterfly book from Theodore Payne Foundation (my go-to resource) but if I look up, say, the yellow butterfly, well, there's like seven different kind that look just like the one that frequents the garden. I just want to maintain the place they are attracted to. There's no need in trying to be an expert.

Rain barrels, compost bin, many hand tools, gloves, wheel barrel, chain saw, rubber boots, straw hat, apron, sun screen and water bottle.

In the book "*Belonging*" by bell hooks, she writes about how the Africans who were stolen and enslaved, came from a rich culture where the land, farming and an inherent know-how to the earth were essential. They continued that practice as slaves. When slavery was officially abolished and the Great Migration began, working the land and slavery were synonymous in their minds. The Great Migration was not only a symbolic move toward freedom but a move away from Ruralism and with that working with the land.

What took the place of working the land? What in the urban vernacular could afford that which working the land inherently provided? With no or very little daily experience to the land, to the earth the connection to ancient culture or a holistic life style was compromised. hooks writes, the re-connection to land is an essential part to the health of the African-American and their culture; re-establishing the connection of earth to human, this bond; re-own it.

Of course, we can see similar trends or close to the same for most immigrant populations in our Nation. Cultural assimilation and the dis-engagement to the soil is where alienation of the alien nation begins. It is part of the cultural vocabulary that is forgotten or abandoned. From this transition or erosion, we start to see a cause and effect detrimental to mental and physical health. This makes for a perfect breeding ground for denial, disempowerment, disenfranchisement, and disconnection. If access is power then this non-relationship to the soil may be a gateway toward the colonized mind and a culture-less and powerless mindset. This is the methodology of colonization.

My privileged situation; having enough land in the City to cultivate a butterfly sanctuary in my backyard is something I highly appreciate. I know it. However, more and more, my friends and community are becoming aware of the benefit and more importantly, the need to cultivate the soil as a life practice essential to health. In fact, many artists see it as a political act, a progressive statement and perhaps an extension of their art practice.

Certainly, the Southern California drought we've witnessed for the past several years made way for this trend but we would be ignorant if we were to begin to think we have started anything. The home garden movement has always existed. There are many government campaigns, non-profits, classes, community gardens and most importantly, just families who have always had something growing on their property as common practice, especially and perhaps solely in lower income/lower middle-class neighborhoods.

Danny Gamboa (Ghost Bikes LA) was telling me about how he project-managed an initiative in Long Beach in the Cambodian community. There were so many vegetables that were not available at local markets for traditional Cambodian dishes, so they raised money for box gardens to be installed in-between the apartment complexes where many Cambodian immigrants lived. The elders cultivated the gardens, taught the younger populations how to get involved and free Cambodian essential vegetables were made available to the community for free.

Ron Finley, the Guerilla Gardener, just south of my neighborhood (Koreatown) has become the spokes-person for neighborhood gardening empowerment. With a couple of TED Talks under his belt, what started as a local initiative with like-minded urbanists in South Central has become an international campaign. In fact, he and his crew were able to get the LA City Council to change the law regarding gardening in the city-owned partition between side-walks and the street.

In 2016, the Los Angeles Cultural Affairs Department launched its first public art biennial. Current L.A. which celebrated the river with a citywide curation of art interventions and programming. With an eclectic roster of innovative artists, one of which was "Ties that Bind" by Mel Chin, the City was infused with colorful art engagements. I volunteered for Mel's initiative; dedicate an 18' x 18' plot on your property to one of his custom local landscape designed drought tolerant/butterfly friendly gardens. Conceptually, the city would have a patchwork of these squares to create paths for butterflies while also promoting drought tolerant/indigenous flora/fauna.

Perhaps one of the more colorful art groups to come out of L.A. is Fallen Fruit, who have been commissioned by many public art agencies to spearhead gardens, orchards and landscapes within new government projects with artistic flare and participatory impulse. I especially appreciate their namesake program where they have these community preserve gatherings. You're supposed to gather fruit that has fallen from fruit trees in your neighborhood and bring them at these events and then they'll help your turn them into jams/preserves. It's art. It's culinary programming. It's social activism.

Time. No one has time and everyone is busy. Sometimes I hear someone respond that they have no gardening talent. Perhaps they tried in the past and everything died. This is where drought tolerant and indigenous plants really come in handy. They require little maintenance and are very difficult to kill. Again, I am fairly clueless to the specifics of growing anything in a garden and yet, I have one in my backyard. Yes, there's a level of education and commitment to get it going but once the plants are set, they require very little work. You also don't necessarily need a plot of land. You can do it in pots or a raised garden. There's much online to learn from including entertaining videos on YouTube. Start small and thematic. Pace yourself and have fun.

What I've learned, having maintained this thing in my backyard for several years now, is this:

A garden teaches you that either you grow or you die.

NOTE: *March 4, 2019, I learned that the State of California officially announced that the drought is over (for now)*

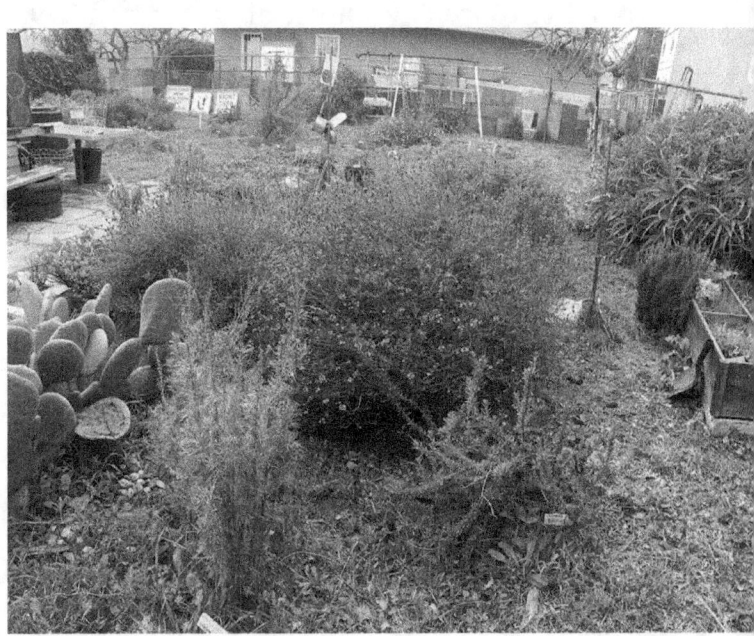

ALAN NAKAGAWA/ GREAT STREETS/ ART PROGRAM

FINAL REPORT/ CONTRACT NO. C-129006

In May of 2017, I was recruited as the Artist Consultant for the Los Angeles Great Streets Program. We had seven projects all together. Three infrastructure projects and four pop ups. Each community was granted funds to engage their communities on awareness raising pop ups of build out solutions that addressed traffic challenges along their main streets. In most cases, these are communities that have been building their base support and coalitions for several years. Our team, made up of City staff, MIG, LA Mas and myself, were to support the communities proposed scope of work. We designed a bottom up approach, where the communities were calling the shots and we were here to support them.

I was given a stipend and each project had a small art budget. The stipend was to pay for my consulting or art expertise and anything above and beyond that was to be covered by the art budget, i.e. equipment, materials, fabrication, delivery, installation etc.

The following is a summary of each of the seven projects:

1) POP UP: 4TH STREET/ PROYECTO PASTORAL
EVENTS:
April 21, 2017: Street Sign Making Workshop: Proyecto Pastoral invited community members for a three-hour participatory art project. Members posed as the "crosswalking street icon" in front of a backlit screen. Local photographer Rafael Cardenas was hired to document each pose. Members of local art collective Ni Santas were hired through local art non-profit Self-Help Graphics to art direct the session. Youth customized Luche Libre coloring sheets.

May 3, 2017: Delivered one dozen sign panels to Self-Help Graphics for Ni Santas to transfer photo images from the April 21st event.

May 6, 2017: Pop Up event at 4th/ Gless Ave.. Temporarily installed one dozen custom street crossing signs. Ni Santas conducted a stencil project with local youth. Youth customized Luche Libre coloring sheets.

DESCRIPTION: America Aceves/Proyecto Pastoral was our main point of contact. She suggested the custom pedestrian crossing signage at our second meeting. Bringing in legendary arts non-profit Self-Help Graphics was discussed, although Proyecto Pastoral had never worked with them in the past. This seemed like a great opportunity. We agreed that I would walk over and see if they would join the campaign. In recent years, Self-Help Graphics had moved two blocks east of Proyecto Pastoral, had recently been enthralled in the Save Boyle Heights controversy, and had recently completed major renovation at their new site. Joel Garcia at Self-Help was more than willing to work with us and introduced us to Ni Santas. Joan Zeta was my point of contact and we were in business. We both new Rafa Cardenas, a well-respected East L.A. photographer who had recently had an exhibition at Espacio 1830. Rafa joined the campaign a week later.

America/Proyecto Pastoral was able to rally a large number of local residents to join us on April 21 at the Youth Technology Center for the sign making session. We had over sixty in attendance and there was a very festive atmosphere all night.

I arranged a field trip to the LADOT sign shop with Ni Santas. We met City staff to discuss how they make street signage for the City.

Rafa processed the silhouette images which we delivered to Ni Santas. I fabricated the mobile signs and sign plates. They were delivered to Self-Help Graphics. Ni Santas was able to complete the stenciled images on time.

On the morning of the Pop Up event, we picked up the completed mobile signs and installed them along 4th Street in time for the Great Streets Pop Up Event. After the Pop Up event, we delivered them to Proyecto Pastoral for them to keep and use for future events.

The signage is now installed as decorative sculpture in and around Proyecto Pastoral's campus.

FOLLOW UP/ DOCUMENTATION:

https://www.alannakagawa.com/#/proyecto-pastoral-great-streets/

https://vimeo.com/216716183

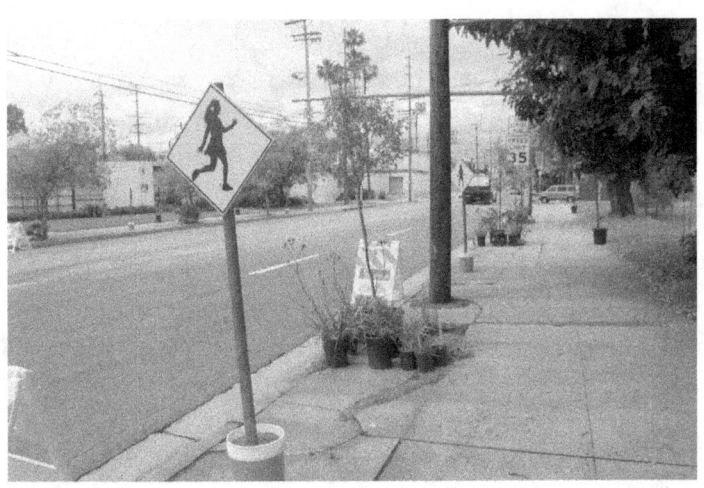

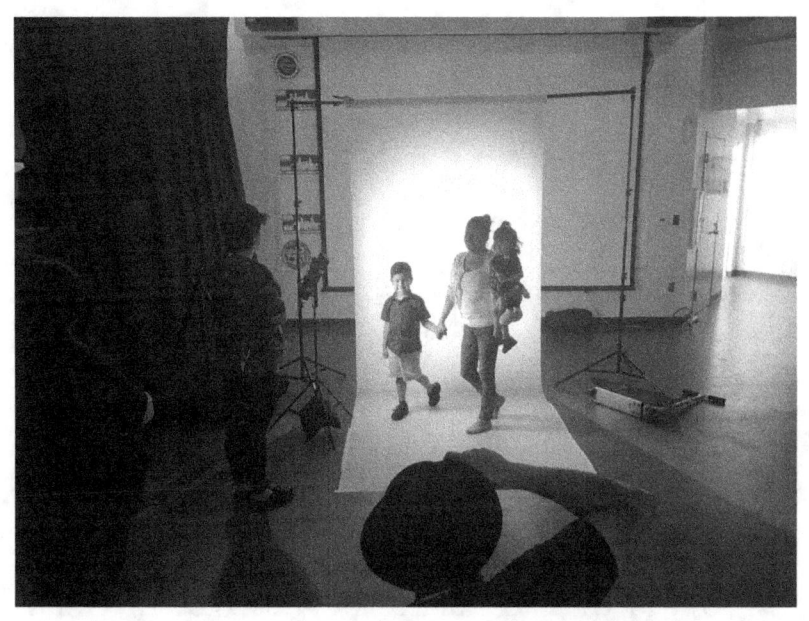

2) POP UP: WILMINGTON/ WATTS REIMAG-
INED
EVENTS:
Pop Up: September 20, 2017, Wilmington Avenue

DESCRIPTION:
This project was challenging. On one hand, you
had an active local organization, Watts Reimagined, wanting to address the need for improvements
along Wilmington Avenue and on the other hand,
this organization, for some reason, was reluctant to
partner with Watts Towers Art Center, a long-stand-
ing City of L.A. art center, located directly in the
center off the Wilmington Ave corridor we were
addressing. I found this to be highly problematic.
Watts Reimagined's very own icon is the Towers. It's

on their letterhead. There seemed to be some local organizational conflict. So, I promised to be part of their Pop Up, which was a lot of fun. I brought my community participatory sound piece, "Sound Forest" and created a coloring sheet were people were asked to draw a future street sign for their neighborhood.

In conjunction with the Pop Up, I was given permission to work with the Watts Towers Art Center on a separate project. I had two meetings with the Watts Towers Art Center Artist In Residents. We decided to use some of the art budget for a start-up podcast project; a Watts Towers Radio Series.

3) POP UP: CRENSHAW BLVD./ WEST ANGELES EVENTS:
August 26, 2017, Pop Up event on Crenshaw Blvd.

DESCRIPTION:
From the get go, the team wanted to do a movie screening event. By the time the date and logistics were set, MIG asked that I bring Sound Forest, which was very comfortable for me to do. In hindsight, I wish I could have worked with the West Angeles folks more. The movie they featured was about the game of chess and how it became the vehicle of empowerment for a community in Uganda. It's been well documented that there's been a longstanding chess club meeting in Leimert Park. I met with the chess club one afternoon at the local McDonalds. It would have taken at least two months to cultivate a relationship with this local institution. I would have

wanted to design a chess set that incorporated local imagery and then at the Pop Up, invite the club to come and play chess on these prototypes and potentially, have a teaching component for kids to learn how to play chess. There just wasn't enough time to instigate this type of project. Regardless, the Pop Up went well.

4) POP UP: HOLLYWOOD BLVD./ THAI CDC
EVENTS:
September 23, 2017, Pop Up on Hollywood Blvd.

DESCRIPTION:
The idea of a mural and specifically to resurrect Vibul Wonparasat's mural formerly on Bangkok Market, (in the original L.A. Thai neighborhood on Melrose Avenue.) came up during the first meeting with Thai CDC, partly due to a twenty-six year reunion between Thai CDC Director Chancee Martorell and I. We were the project managers of that mural and agreed that it was highly unfortunate that the mural had been white-washed due to maintenance problems. I was able to hire the original producers of the mural, the Social and Public Art Resource Center (SPARC) to create a large digital print of the work on archival canvas. Using C-Stands, the artwork was installed at the Pop Up. We arranged for Thai CDC to take ownership of the work in hopes that they will continue to feature it at future events in the community.

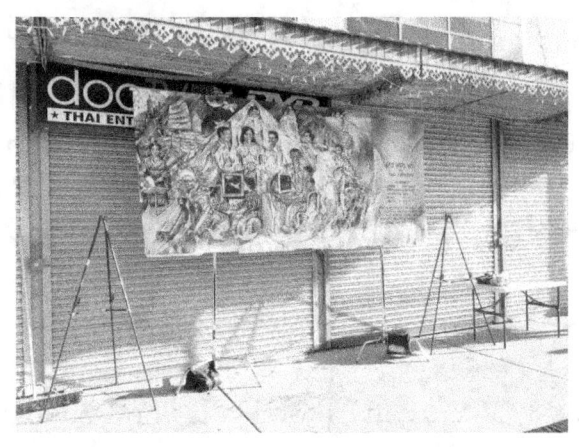

5) INFASTRUCTURE: PICO BLVD./ PICO BLVD.
GREAT STREETS
EVENTS:
February 15, 2017, Zine Workshop #1
March 3, 2017, Zine Workshop #2
April 8, 2017, Zine Workshop #3
May 4, 2017, Pick up printed zines at PiperTech.
Deliver zines to Pico Blvd GS team
May 4, 2017, Zine It On Pico launch at Rosalind's,
1044 S Fairfax Avenue L.A. CA 90019
May 6, 2017, Spring Fling Community Event, Distribute Zines
June 23, 2017, Met with Committee members to
brainstorm about a utility box project
May 1, 2018, Remaining funds will be used for an
art project TBD at the KABOOM pocket park along
Hauser Blvd and Pico Blvd in the future.

DESCRIPTION:
After meeting with the Pico Blvd. Great Streets

Committee Members, we found out that there was a large artist population living in the neighborhood as informally surveyed by committee members and local neighborhood galleries. Yet, a project or event had not been created to draw the artists together. This was step one in our initial process. At the first meeting of over twenty artists convened. After some discussion, we agreed on using the zine making process as a way to solicit local artists to offer ideas of future public art projects for the corridor. The zine was titled Zine It On Pico. A Facebook site was created and has become the gathering place for additional projects for the artistic community along this corridor. Zine It On Pico has been used as a way to solicit the community for project support and involvement in the overall Pico Blvd Great Streets project.

As of April 2018, a decrease in the art budget was communicated and therefore this project saw up to $2,000 less in the budget. The remaining budget will be used by the committee to paint utility boxes along the corridor.

FOLLOW UP/ DOCUMENTATION:

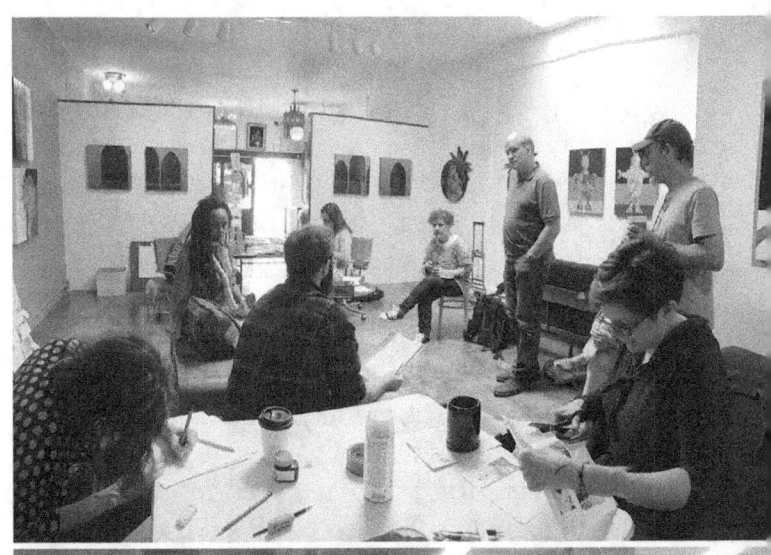

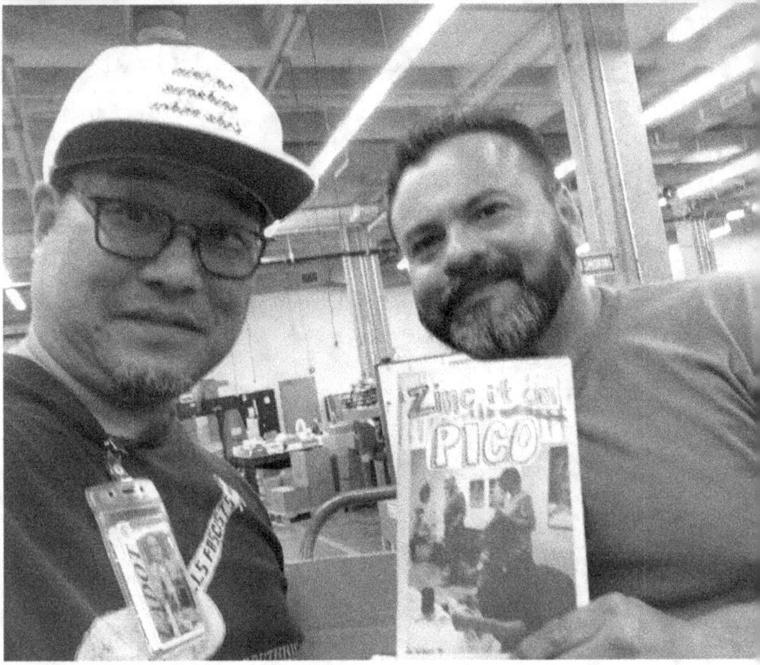

6) INFASTRUCTURE: ROBERTSON BLVD./ SOUTH ROBERTSON

EVENTS:

April 13, 2017, I met with members of the SORO Great Streets Committee and we brainstormed several ideas about public art projects for the corridor.

June 4, 2017, SORO Block Party. Illustrations of various public art ideas were presented with a request for community comments. Sound Forest was available for the general public.

February 20, 2018, it was decided that we will move forward with a crosswalk painting project

April 28, 2018, A site visit of artist painted crosswalks in Pasadena with artist Hataya Tubtim

May 16, 2018, A presentation of the conceptual crosswalk painting will be presented to the LADOT Complete Streets meeting

May 1, 2018, LADOT approved the crosswalk art design by Nakagawa. Implementation of the artwork will be part of the construction project. Schedule TBD

DESCRIPTION:

Outreach during the block party was great. I met a lot of people including Mayor Garcetti. The Sound Forest attracted a lot of families. Parents would just wait while their kids played the sculptures. That gave me an opportunity to speak with the parents and have them respond to public art options for the corridor which were illustrated on boards on easels next to the Sound Forest.

During research for the painted crosswalk, LADOT

shared the paint store that supplied the colors of the Broad crosswalk. The paint is very temporary. A year after its installation, the paint is approximately 30% chipped away due to vehicular traffic. One can argue that Robertson is equally as congested during rush hours. I recommend we only do the East and West sides and not the walkway that crosses Robertson.

As of April 2018, a decrease in the art budget was communicated and therefore this project saw up to $2,000 less in the budget.

FOLLOW UP/ DOCUMENTATION:
Video: https://vimeo.com/220425430
Password: Soundforest

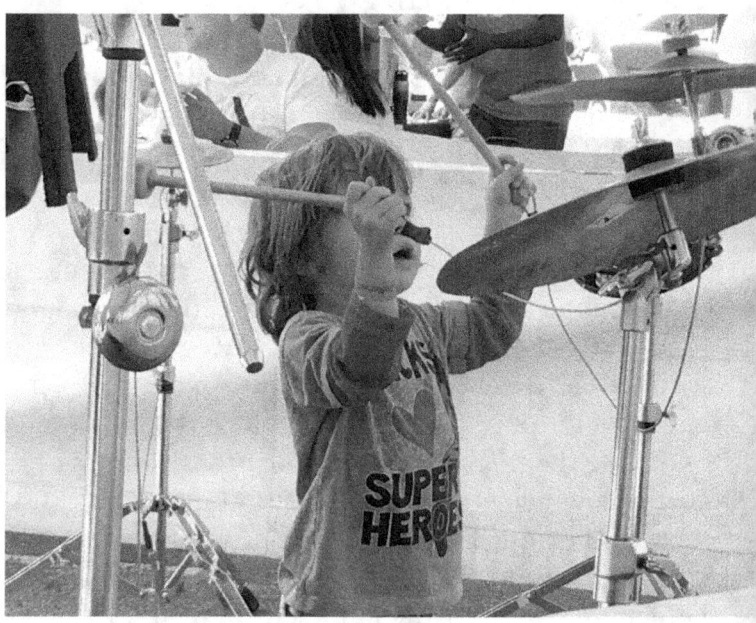

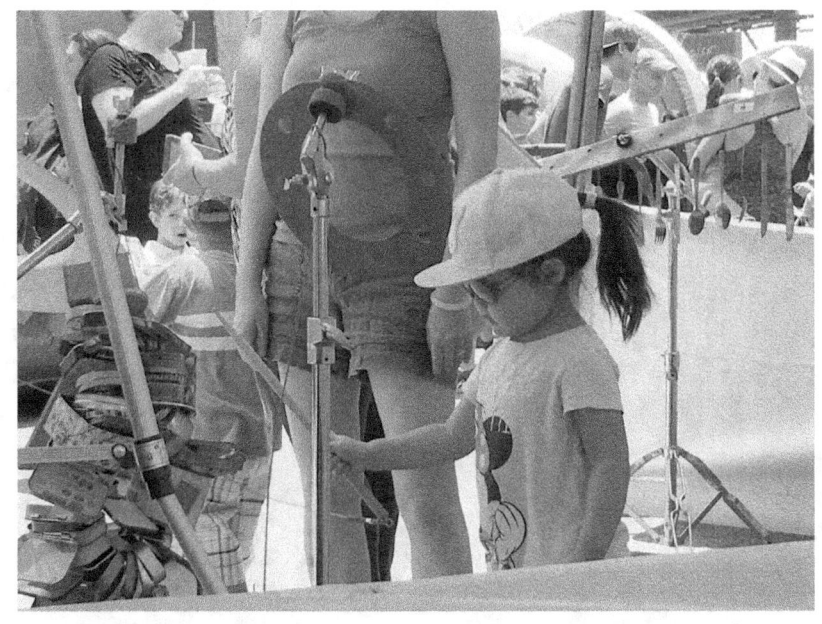

7) INFASTRUCTURE: VAN NUYS BLVD./ PA-CIOMA BEAUTIFUL
EVENTS:
May 30, 2017, Zine Workshop at Pacoima Public Library with Teen Program
October 3, 2017, Team decides artwork will be a recreating of a historic signage
March 12, 2018, Site visit to determine location of sign
April 23, 2018, Pending final approval to move forward with signage design, engineering and fabrication
May 1, 2018, An art signage project will be part of construction phase on either the traffic island or the pocket park in front of the proposed street closure.

DESCRIPTION:

The team decided that the historic or related sign would be the art project.

As of April 2018, a decrease in the art budget was communicated and therefore this project saw up to $2,000 less in the budget.

GREAT STREETS CREATIVE PROGRAMMING TOOL

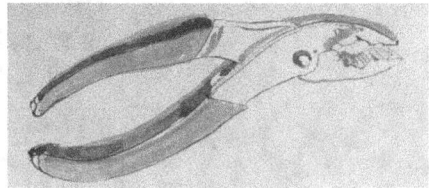

Introduction

In 2016, I was the Creative Catalyst/Artist In Residence for the Los Angeles Department of Transportation. During this twelve-month project, I met with Great Streets staff who invited me to become the Creative Consultant for Great Streets (2017-18). It was introduced to me that this would be an experiment of sorts but that I would have the opportunity to consult with each of the seven Great Streets (GS) community-based teams and help them develop an art component that met their needs.

My job description: Great Streets Creative Consultant is responsible for facilitating pathways for artistic, cultural, and creative representation in each Great Streets Challenge project.

This document is in response to this Deliverable in my contract: "*...develop/produce a tool for the*

Great Streets Challenge to use for future program years to ensure that design, art and culture are a routine accommodation incorporated into projects of the Great Streets Challenge;"

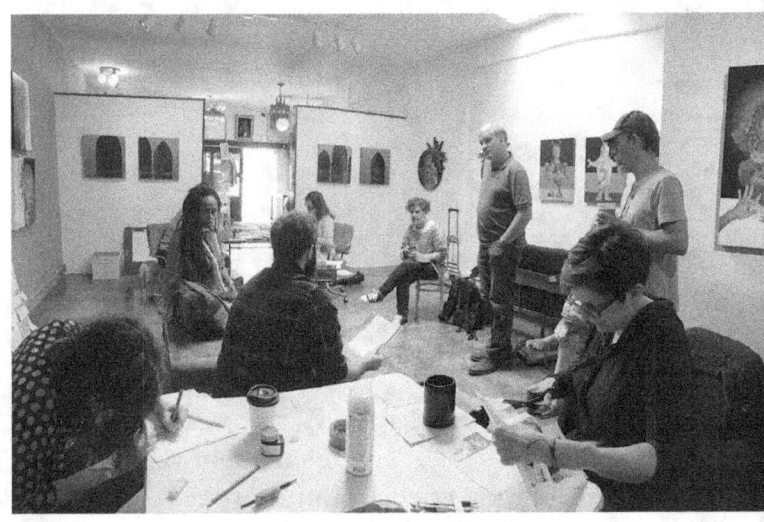

Zine it On Pico workshop/ Pico Blvd Great Streets

It's difficult, for me, to create a meaningful document/tool without getting too much into the minutiae or on the other hand get so general that it communicates nothing. How can I make this worth your time and more importantly, helpful? Also, I don't see myself as a writer per se. I'm a sound artist, actually. In the past, I've been part of the making of many government documents but honestly, it's not my style or expertise to author something like a policy recommendation, board report or a master plan. So, if it's alright with you, I'd like to tackle this puzzle more like a letter, from one artist to another.

Starting, Generally Speaking

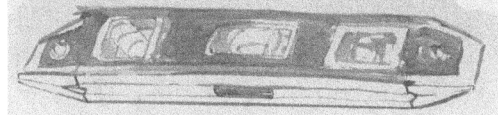

At the start of each of the seven Great Streets projects I participated in, there were common key points I discussed with the each of the GS community project liaisons;
-What are the key needs we need to address?
-Is there an existing arts community participating and/or existing in the project area?
-Who will be affected by this project?

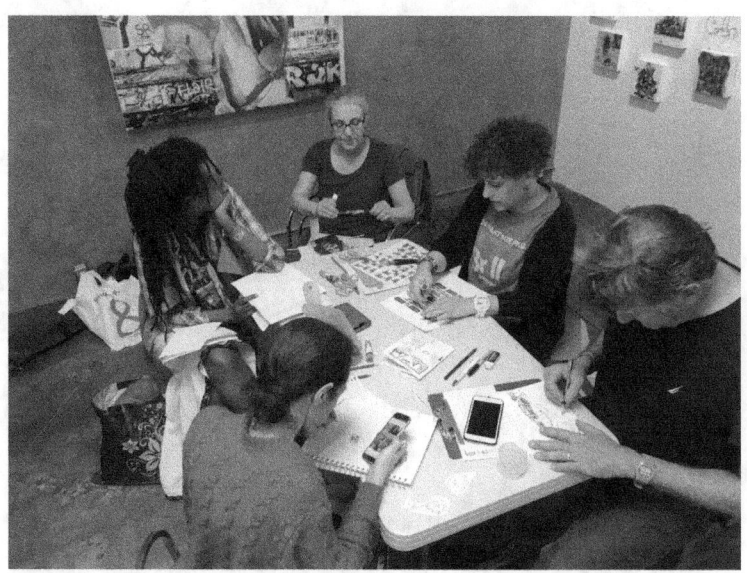

Zine it On Pico workshop/ Pico Blvd Great Streets

What are the key needs we need to address?
Although this is described extensively in their project description, when an artist asks this question, the community will inevitably re-answer with an arts/culture slant. This may be a good opportunity for you to learn if the community members have given thought to what type of art they had already envisioned. This is not necessarily the path the project will take but it's a good way to establish where they are coming from, what level of community arts/culture they have been exposed to and what sort of arts/culture language exists already. As the Creative Consultant, this can help establish common ground, expectations and possibly where the opportunities to build on existing art/culture ideas, processes and possibilities lay.

Is there an existing arts community participating and/or existing in the project area?
Obviously, the answer to this can lead the way to various advantages. For instance, if there is an existing artist or arts collective or arts organization, it's a good idea to find out what the relationship is with the community and project leaders. On one project, I was told that the GS project members had never worked with an art non-profit that I knew was in the same neighborhood. After speaking about them at one meeting, it was decided that they would be open to working with them in the context of their GS project, which turned out to be a very positive experience. On another GS project, I was told that there was a local artist but they would prefer to open the project to new artists because the community

group had done so many projects with this one artist in the past and felt it was time to diversify their artist experiences. There was one GS project where the community group was well aware of artists in the community but had never tried to get them together. We decided to use the GS project to create workshops were information could be shared but also to have an opportunity where the artists in the neighborhood could meet each other.

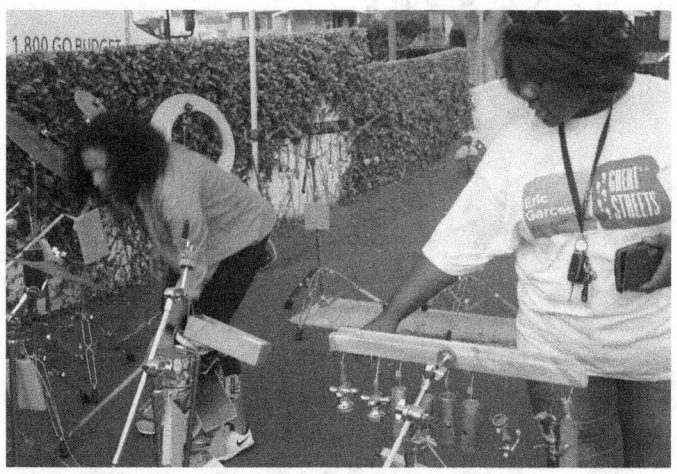

Sound Forest/ West Angeles Great Streets Pop Up

Who will be affected by this project?
There are the GS Team members, the community folks who make up the GS Challenge grant recipients and the greater community/users. It is the latter that is so often the difficult population to foresee but it's important because often the community members don't think about the "greater good" beyond

their immediate community, when in fact, the users of any project will include the greater City population. This is very important when it comes to the art/cultural component(s) because it's your job to always make sure that what's being created in the "silo" of the granted community will have meaning to the greater population.

Medium and Flexibility

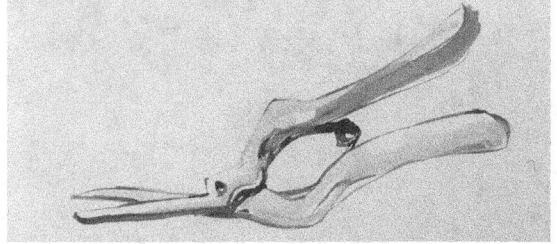

When I was the A.I.R. for LADOT, I thought I got the project, which was a National call, because of my experience in transportation (working for the LA Metro's Metro Art program). Towards the end of my LADOT residency, I made a comment to that affect to Seleta Reynolds, LADOT's General Manager. She was quick to reply with, "That's not why we selected you. We selected you because you listen." Well, of course, that could probably be debated by a number of my family members and former relationships but that aside, I am a sound artist. Listening and all of its nuances is my greatest fascination. I have worked on consensus building with a diverse array of communities throughout LA County.

I received Oral History training at UCLA. Listening is key. Of course, asking the right questions is key as well but when working with the GS community teams, listening was paramount.

In most cases, these communities have been working on their respective improvements for years and in some cases, decades. They are volunteers, who have invested money and time towards the objectives they state in their GS Applications. It takes so much to get to the level where you can even apply for Great Streets. In other words, you are walking into a rich and vibrant culture and your job is to hit the ground running, while being flexible, compassionate and pro-active with a healthy dose of patience, selflessness and accommodation. Beyond the cliché government process descriptive of "hurry up and wait," these communities each have a pace of their own and that combined with governments pace can lead to spacious gaps between milestones. Do what you need to do to survive because by taking on this project, you are in it for the "long haul," especially the "Build" projects.

Being flexible is part of working with communities and I suspect you already know that and most likely have experience in that, so I'd like to touch on a different angle to this with two stories.

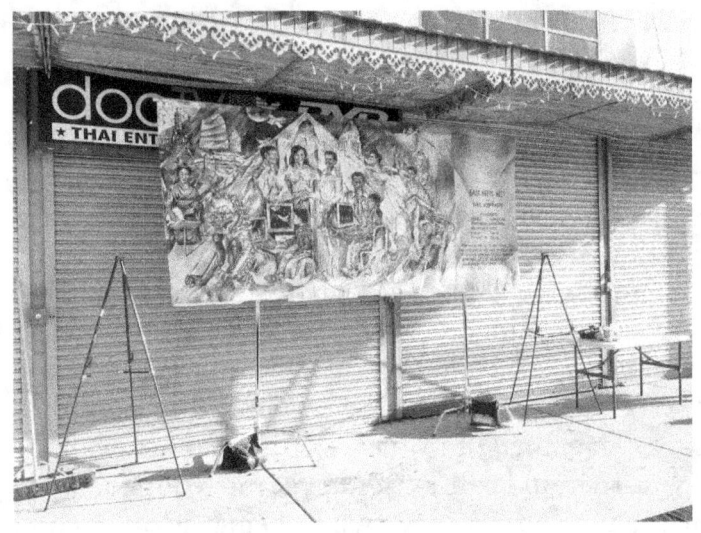

Vibul Wonprasat/ SPARC; Thai CDC Great Street Pop Up

Story #1

I am so grateful for the GS administrative staff for their flexibility, specifically on the Wilmington GS Pop Up. Wilmington Ave is the busy street that runs immediately east of Watts Towers Art Center but for some reason they were not participating in our community outreach and quite frankly, there seemed to be some reluctance to reach out to them above and beyond the emails that were being sent to the general community, so of course I had breakfast with them.

I am a big fan of the Watts Towers Art Center and the cultural legacy it represents. I'm also a fan of the Watts Coffee House, so, I met an Art Center staff Raisha Wilcots there one Sunday afternoon and on discussing what GS was doing and what the Art Center needs were, I learned much about the history of urban improvements in the community.

The merits of a Pop Up's aside, the Watts Art Center was asking if there was anything we could do that would have a longer life span than a Pop Up. Next, I met with some of the Watts Towers A.I.R.s. They have an extensive multi-disciplinary roster of artists in residence. I proposed back to GS staff if I could take a portion of the art budget and instigate a Watts Towers podcast project. The Art Center had the staff experience, technological capability and will to produce an on-going podcast series that would highlight the cultural equity of the community in and around Wilmington Ave. Of course, I produced art programming for our Pop Up but in addition to that, the podcast series was something everyone could look forward to long after our successful four-hour event.

Story #2

Social Practice in the arts has been around for decades and yet it is still not widely understood. Case in point, when I was selected for the LADOT project, I was told that there were five finalists and I got the highest scores, so, I was hired first. Initially, there was an intention to hire as many of the remaining four artist/artist teams in addition to what I was tasked to do. Around the sixth month of my residency, I was told that they were in fact going to move forward with one of the four artist(s) finalists. Not too much after that, I was invited to review their proposal. I came to find out that the LADOT staff actually didn't like their project as is because they wanted more of a connection to the community or neighborhood it was being proposed in, which in this case was a busy intersection in Downtown LA, with a complicated population made up of businesses and residents. (There had been a rise in mix-use development in recent years and so these were all new and fairly affluent residents.) It was decided to go back to the artist and ask them if they could work with the community to revise their proposal so that it would be more site-specific. About a month later, I asked one of the engineers how that was going and they said it was dropped because the artist stated that they did not want to work with the community.

So, two things. One, this was a finalist. What would have happened if this artist got a higher score than me and became the LADOT A.I.R.? How did this artist get so far in the selection process? Why would an artist apply for this project when they don't like working with communities? Secondly, this brings up the topic of perception. The artist perceived that her/his/their concept had enough merit so that any counter process or input was unnecessary and so she/he/they had a "take it or leave it" methodology. Regarding Social Practice and more specifically GS, this is the antithesis of the type of mindset we need. Our goal must be win-win, with no exceptions.

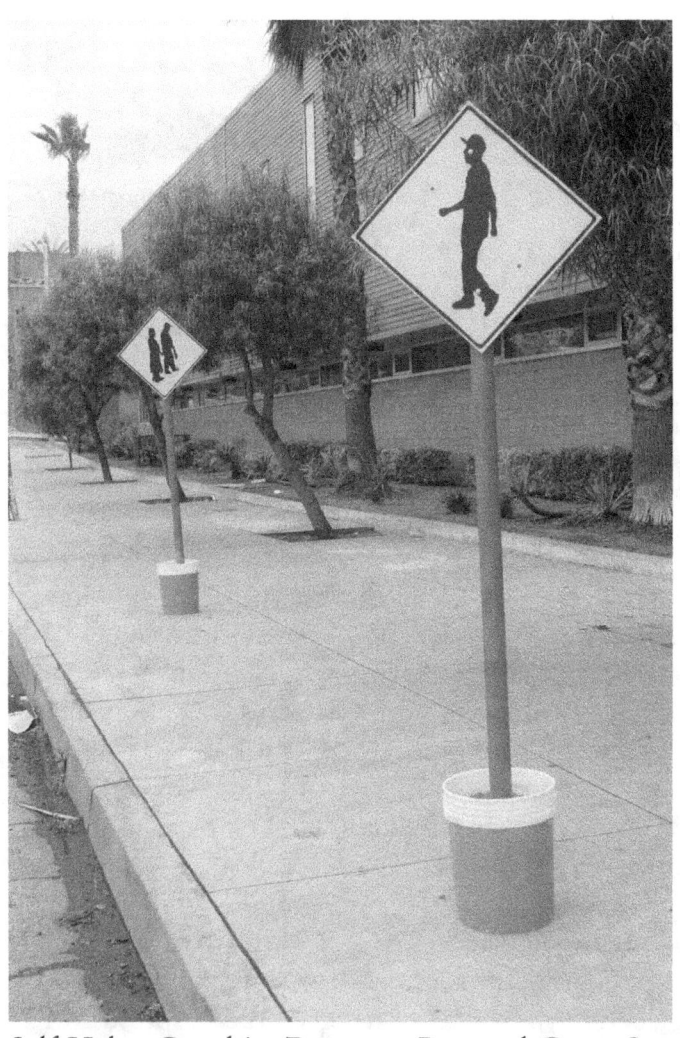

Self Helps Graphics/Proyecto Pastoral Great Streets
Pop Up

Medium

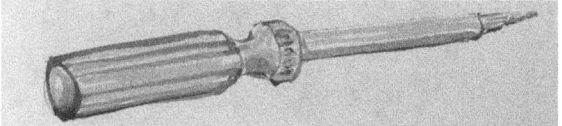

I am going to assume that you are well versed in a variety of media and materials. Each community has its own history of public art, some more than others but everyone has an idea of what is possible. We must listen to what everyone has to share. We then can present alternative ideas, histories and solutions.

At the beginning, every possibility should be put on the table, even if it goes against your natural tendencies, even if you have no experience in that media or technology. Think of each idea, each proposal as a slice of the community voice. Everyone should be heard and responded to. The media is like this malleable/tactile common ground in the community process, which brings me to two stories.

Story #1
When I worked at Metro Art, I would often manage the artist selection process for stations or bus projects. More than likely, artist would respond to Request For Qualification's or Request For Proposal's and then through an arts professional and community representative-based selection panel, finalists would be selected.

Those finalists would be paid to create a proposal.

The final panel day would be comprised of each finalist presenting their proposal to the panel and at the end of the day, one proposal would be selected. Often but not always, the proposal with the most amount of material samples, that the artist would pass around and the panelists could "touch" while the artist presented their idea, would receive the commission. There's something about touching a colorful tile or a piece of hand-made glass that really speaks volumes. It's the opportunity for a tactile shared experience that calls upon something basic, almost primitive and opens the door to the creative mindset. We are after-all, building trust, the trust in an artist's creativity.

Budget and Taxes

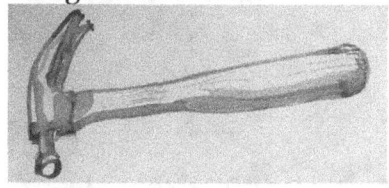

Each Build project was allocated an art budget of $15k and Pop Ups received a budget of $5k each. So that makes for a total of (3)Builds + (4)Pop Ups = $65,000. I received this amount separately in two payments, about 45% of it in 2017 and then 55% in 2018. To my surprise, I had to pay taxes on this amount out of my own pocket because by the time I figured all that out, we had spent all the money from the first check on the projects. It was close to $4,000. I'd never had to pay that much for my taxes. It was shocking. Build it into your budget from day one. When I received the second check, I had to take out 20% for taxes which severely decreased the amount for each art project but that's what you have to do. This is something you need to really keep in mind as you build your budget.

Recently, I had an exhibition at the Orange County Museum of Art. They gave me a project budget in addition to an artist stipend. They were more than happy to order supplies and equipment against my project budget. In this way, as a non-profit, they did not need to pay taxes on those goods the way I would have if I had received the total amount and purchased supplies and equipment on my own. It's convoluted, I know, but please be aware of these types of details. Perhaps speaking with a tax specialist would be a good idea.

CONCLUSION

As an experiment the GS project lead to many new experiences for me. Each project presented a different set of challenges and opportunities but I hope these notes have helped you in some way. What you'll experience may be and most likely will be completely different from what I experienced. That is the exciting reality of this program and this unique gig. Understand the possibilities and the capabilities of each circumstance. Congratulations on being selected and I wish you the best of luck with your new job.

Alan Nakagawa
Creative Catalyst/Artist In Residence, 2017-2018

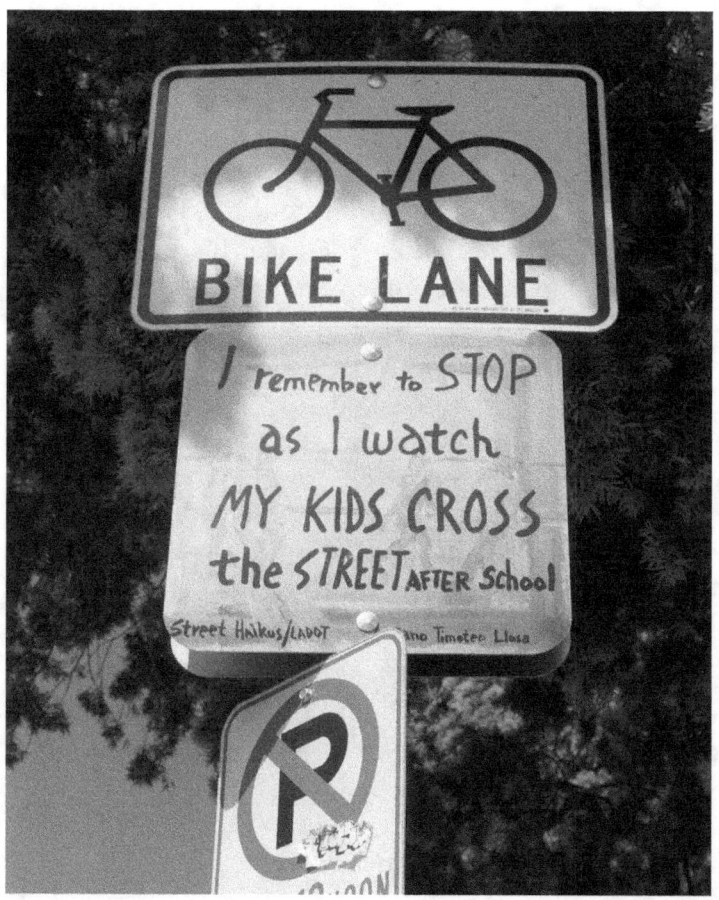

Street Haiku's/ Mar Vista Great Streets

JUNE 11, 2019

Wow, I think I had three hours sleep
It's 6:36 AM and I've been awake since 2:30 AM.
Today is going to be rough.

In any field that your heart is into, you want to do more than you're asked. I guess that's better than ending up doing more than you're asked in a field you don't care for, often the case. It's important to be passionate about what you do.

I've been rolling around in my head about a community project I was asked to participate in. I met with the organizers on the site they wanted me to propose a sound piece. The site has sensitive history regarding the internment of Japanese-Americans during world war II. I met with the Japanese-American community representatives and I designed a project I thought was feasible and compassionate.

A week since they accepted my proposal, here are the pros and cons that kept me from sleeping.

PROS
It's for a one-day huge event

The site is sacred and historical

The contact is someone I've worked well within the past

The community is important to me and historically overlooked

This would be an appropriate event for one of my pop-up projects

I am now in contact with this JA community

It could be a good opportunity to work with the students I am currently working with

CONS
I was contacted a little over a 6 weeks before the event (I would think this type of event would take at least 8 months to organize)

 The organizers want to put vendors and food trucks on the historic site

There's no budget, which means they expect me to pay for some of the expenses as well as work for free and develop a new work for free

The whole event smells like a project that's exploiting the arts community for economic development

Given this gut feeling, it would be irresponsible of me to participate in something that I often have lectured against; exploiting artists

Given this gut feeling, it would be irresponsible of me to invite the students to participate

June 13, 2019 (continuation of process)
Dear (events organizer) and (community representatives),
I appreciate the effort that's been put in the up-coming (community event) and the emails recently exchanged about the efforts pertaining to my proposal. Thank you for all your hard work.

My intentions are to move forward with the plan we discussed but I'd like to make clear why I've decided to move forward without getting compensated.

On May 22, I was invited to participate in the (this event) specifically to propose a sound-based work in front of the (historic site). I requested a meeting at the site. Three days later we met at the site. Realizing the site was actually a memorial, I felt uncomfortable with proposing anything without meeting the members in charge of the memorial. A meeting with (community) committee members took place June 6. By then, I had an idea that tied my project (existing project at university) to the site. This is part of my current artist residency at (university). I felt this was an appropriate path forward because one, the (my project at the university) (have a history with the subject matter of the historic site) and two, the corner of (location) is generally too loud for a sound work due to traffic.

I have mixed feelings about not being compensated as an artist because I think there's a history of organizations assuming artists don't have to be compensated. Furthermore, I feel that there are many projects created across the Nation that are guised as community art but rarely have the intentions of benefiting the artists. There's an idea that artists don't need to get paid. This is tied into the Nations educational system and a common view of the arts. Today, there's a lack of arts education. There's an assumption that artists are bohemians, don't work and/or are not organized, that art itself is a luxury and superfluous. Yet, it's used continuously as a catalyst for communities, commerce and economic development. I am a professional artist. This is not a hobby. I've been trained to become an artist. I make my living as an artist. It wasn't always like this. It took time to get to a place where I could do this full time. In recent years I have received contracts compensating me for my work as an artist with organizations such as LADOT and the Getty Villa and currently with LA County Library, Cal State University Dominguez Hills and the Pasadena Buddhist Temple. In some cases, I applied and in some cases I was invited.

Last year, my friends at 800 Traction Avenue, artists who had lived there since the late 1970's and who paved the way for the neighborhood to becoming the Arts District in DTLA, were evicted. Accordingly, I remember a time when many artists lived in Venice but have since left the community due to rising rent costs. There's much written about artists being "used" for a lack of a better term by land developers to "sweeten" real estate. The question is, who does these art projects benefit?

This experience of the (event) also reminds me of a recent story I learned about that is oddly reflective. I had the honor of interviewing Mitzi Naohara a couple of weeks ago. She is now in her 90's and lives in the facility formerly Keiro in Boyle Heights. During WWII, she and her family were sent to Poston Internment Camp in Arizona. Her husband to be had heard that they were paying people to go to Manzanar and help construct the facility. He went because he couldn't find work in Los Angeles. Mitzi said he worked very hard but after a while he found out he wasn't going to get paid. He ended up leaving, only to be interned at a different camp._Getting paid reflects mutual value in our capitalist economy.

It is an honor to be working with the members of (community). Their work is amazing to me and of course the history they are working to illuminate is vital for the community to recognize. I also have been a fan of (community member) for decades and trust her guidance. As this arts festival moves forward, I feel it's important to represent the intentions of (community) and their voices. I am not convinced that was going to happen. I'm glad it's happening now. That's why I'm moving forward with my proposal.

As I become savvier as a full-time artist, I am learning when to say yes and when to say no to opportunities. I know that I am privileged to have the opportunities I have. In this specific case, I should have asked for clarification if there was budget or not from the initial invitation. It was alluded to but not clear. I trust the experience will be educational and beneficial on some level. Thank you for this opportunity.

(the response by the organizers was prompt and comprehensive. It was an explanation about why artists don't need to get paid)

(the university staff read this response and pulled their students out of the project and encouraged me to do the same, which I did)

(later, I met one of the community members and they said there was no art project at the site the day of the event and the food trucks blocked their memorial. There was a band playing music at the site)

I DON'T CARE

Are there more harmful, hurtful and game ending words than this?

Often, how we enter civic discourse is rooted in our experiences with family.

A memory that is still so resonant to me is when I was in college and was speaking with my Aunt about the growing homeless population in Los Angeles (1983). This may have been in the course of a conversation about her job with the Immigration and Naturalization Service. I may had made a statement to the effect that rather than increasing funding regarding immigration that we should use those funds to help the homeless to which she responded, "Why should we help those people? That's not my responsibility."

Here is the fundamental difference between caring and not caring. Even if you don't do anything- volunteer, donate money and or show any support for people, the least you could have is have some degree of compassion. By stating you don't care, ends the conversation.

I don't care.

I had a similar conversation recently with another family member regarding the current President. We went back and forth on the pros and cons of Trump.

I was con and he was pro but what really struck me was he said he didn't vote, that in fact, he has never voted. I have to admit, that reveal dumfounded me. I almost felt like saying, then what am I doing wasting my time with debating this with you? I care about my Uncle very much and we agree on more than we disagree but I hadn't realized he didn't vote.

What does it mean to not care? In this context. He watches conservative, pro-Trump media and agrees with it all and vilifies the left but when you don't vote, don't really engage in community, don't mentor youth and aren't really educating yourself above and beyond one television channel on cable, then what is the meaning of having such a specific political opinion?

I don't care?

To what degree do you not care?

I'm an artist and I've been privileged to engage in civic discourse. I vote. I mentor. I listen. I document. I participate. I share.

Many see the arts as superfluous. Meaning they see culture as superfluous? Meaning they see voice as superfluous? Meaning they see how they and their community is represented as superfluous? Meaning how their culture is represented as superfluous?

To what degree do you not care?

Do you not care how artists see the world?
Do you not care how they are representing you?

Visual artists, animators, filmmakers, choreographers, writers, poets, composers, critics, philosophers, analysts are all representing our time and place in history. They are invested, in varying degrees, with our communities.

They add to the civic voice and therefore help sculpt how it's not only represented but how it's steered.

I once heard former Secretary of State Condoleezza Rice say that protestors are misinformed. She said that no protest march has ever changed policy. I couldn't believe it. This is a person of power or at least had power at one point. She's a woman. Did the marches for women's right to vote not have an effect on women rights to vote? She is African-American. Did not the freedom Marches have an effect on the Civil Rights Act? What is the process for someone to attain so much power but be so far away from political activism and the power of people?

I was recently with a young Latina photographer who was criticizing the US as a false democracy. She said it is an autocracy and that the celebrating of the US as a democracy is a falsehood. I said while it's true the US is not perfect, it is an experiment of sorts. Last year 47 percent of eligible voters voted. What is the process that leads to less than half voting? Who benefits from this process? There's your autocracy.

The nation's politics is a pendulum theory in action.

The disenfranchised remain so because they are not empowered. They have been trained to not empower themselves and this condition deters voice; their voice and therefore our voice.

Is the Autocracy engineered or is it self-imposed? I think that question is the chicken or the egg. What no one ever mentions about the chicken or the egg is that it's really a smoke screen to draw you away from the fox in the hen house. Who cares what came first. The real question is how do we insure that every egg gets counted, so to speak?

Last year (2018), I had a solo exhibition at the Visitors Welcome Center in Los Angeles. There were two rooms. For one room, I installed a participatory sculpture that was based on the notion of dreaming and immigration. In the other room, I presented artifacts from the various artist in residencies I had participated up to that point.

Regarding the latter, I wanted to celebrate these opportunities in the context of the art gallery I was showing in because I was in part hoping to inspire the community to engage in more civic discourse, to apply to these types of residencies in communities and/or administered by government agencies. Some of the residencies where with community/government organization historically not incorporating the services of an artist, i.e. the L.A. Department of Transportation, the City of L.A. Mayor's Great Streets project.

The interesting aspect of an art gallery or an art museum, is that it is often populated by repeat users, people who have already been acclimated to the benefits of engaging in the arts, or as the saying goes, preaching to the choir. What if out of one hundred gallery/museum visitors we could inspire one artist to begin engaging with the public or work in government? That would be success. During my exhibition, I mentioned this to another artist and he said, "Are you kidding me? Artists, especially those who go to art galleries like this aren't interested in dealing with the public."

Most art programs at universities and colleges are not set up for civic dialogue and public engagement. I recently met with someone who is the director of a civic engagement department at a local art college. He was describing a semester curriculum that was a twelve-session course where the class chooses a community organization to study and propose a project. He went on to say that, at a minimum, one of the classes should take place at the community location. When he said that I didn't know how to react. He was the director of this program. I thought all the sessions should take place in the community. The disconnect between my concept of civic engagement and his was too immense for me. What are the students learning? It illustrated how we as artists who are trained to work with the community have a different mode of operation. It seemed to me that this art college program director was an uninformed client. I think he sees himself as the expert who will tell the community what they need. What a disconnect. In public engagement, the community is the expert. This director and I are working from different paradigms.

If I get introduced or introduce myself to someone at a party and for the first thirty seconds, I can hear them speak but their eyes are scanning the room, we are not having a conversation. We are standing next to each other. We are verbalizing something and the other is maybe hearing but there's no true conversation happening. There is communication. What's being communicated is "I'll stand with you for this moment but as soon as I see someone more important than you I will no longer be standing next to you." In some ways, that's how the head of this art college program was describing their cultural policy. They are the experts. The community is not the experts. We will assess the community and tell them what they need. On a broader level, no one likes to be told what they need because in a way, it's saying we don't care.

1/1/19

As I was growing up in what is now Koreatown in Los Angeles, I lived in an ethnically diverse population but was raised in a Japanese household and community. Ours was not a Japanese-American community, because my family and most family friends were from Japan and primarily from Hiroshima. My family came to the US, specifically LA, in 1957. I was the first US born in my family and was the only kid for the first five years until my brother Carl was born.

From the late 1960's to the early 1980's, my parents owned a restaurant called Beni Basha, which was located on the northeast corner of Norton Ave and Olympic Blvd. At first, most customers were Japanese families but towards the end it had a very diverse clientele. This was during a time when few Americans knew what sushi was if you could imagine that. It was pre-*Shogun* (based on a James Clavell novel), the television series that changed it all for Japanese-Americans but that's another story.

Back then, I recall a big green grocery van would stop in our neighborhood off Pico Blvd and Crenshaw Ave. There was one grocer inside, Japanese with a white apron and black rubber boots. This van had steps leading into the interior, which was a mini-market. Inside, Japanese housewives would buy Spanish Mackerel, rice, tofu, natto, red miso, Nappa cabbage, Daikon (Japanese radish), etc. and I would always eye the candies from Japan; Glico caramel with the illustration of an Olympic runner on it or Milky with the cartoon of a girl with really big eyes (the precursor to Yoshitomo Nara's characters).

All our family friends were from Japan with kids like me who were born in the US. My family was the Japanese restaurant folks. Back then, there were several Japanese restaurants up and down Olympic Blvd. One of my fondest childhood memories was going to one of the movie theaters in our neighborhood to watch films from Japan. The theaters would ask to put their posters in our restaurant window and in exchange we got free movie tickets. I would go to see these films with my parents and squirm uncomfortably during the sex scenes, laugh during the comedies like *Otoko-wa-tsurai-yo* but was most fixated with the Samurai movies like *Zato-ichi the blind swordsman* or films based on the historic warrior, Miyamoto Musashi.

Every summer, someone would come to visit from Japan, which is how I came to know so many family members from there. As I look back, no one ever talked about how things were in Japan. They more marveled about being in the US and primarily Disneyland or Hollywood. I realize now that most of these grand uncles and aunts witnessed the war on some level. They were the survivors of a brutal war, the citizens of a country that bombed Pearl Harbor, terrorized Asia but inevitably lost the war. The country was re-tooling into an economic industrial giant. My family was an example of the American Dream and the Japanese diaspora. There was always this inherent tension. Who was better off? Those who stayed in Japan or those who left Japan?

So many times, my family would offer to send me to visit Japan. What? I was "American." Why would I want to go to Japan? It was part of my stubbornness, rebellion and ignorance. I was arrogant and spoiled. "No" was always a power move on my part but little did I know it was actually the result of my colonized mind. I was conditioned to think that anything Japanese was backwards and unworthy of any of my time. At some point, Japanese television became available on the weekends. The family would crowd around the living room to watch it and I remember how embarrassed I was about what was being televised. Somehow, I had adopted a shame complex of this post war culture across the Pacific. I rejected anything Japanese and in many ways rejecting myself. This conflict would last well into my mid-twenties, until I finally went to Japan.

Around 1987, I was completing my MFA at UC Irvine, when one day my Grandmother handed me an advertisement she had cut out of the Rafu Shimpo, the LA-based Japanese community newspaper. It was an announcement of the Monbusho Scholarship. The Monbusho is Japan's Ministry of Education and Culture. The scholarship is open to post graduates who want to do research in a specific field that is unique to Japan. It was all expenses paid with a monthly stipend for up to two years. My Grandmother did not like my girlfriend at the time so she wanted me to leave the country and the woman I was living with. My grandmother was the most powerful person in my family and she made me promise that I would apply. I was selected for the Monbusho and my Grandmother got her way, with everything.

It was 1988. It was my first time in Japan. It was my first time living outside the US. It was my first time experiencing four seasons. It was my first time living in a homogeneous society. In was my first time living in a non-English speaking environment.

My first stop was six months at Osaka University of Foreign Language in Mino Osaka. This is where Monbusho scholars were sent if they didn't speak Japanese or not enough to go directly to the university they were assigned to. It was located on a mountain-side on the outskirts of the city center. I remember my first-time riding on a bus from the university to the train station to get to downtown Osaka. I was sitting in the bus and suddenly came to this realization that it was the first time my body fit perfectly in the bus seat. I am short in America but taller than my parents. In Japan, everything is designed for my size or shorter. It never occurred to me how everything in Los Angeles was not intended for my body size. This was where my mind began to change, "decolonize," although I wasn't aware of this term at that time.

In 2018, I was invited to become the artist-in-residence for the Ninomiya Photography Archive, California State University Dominguez Hills. An amazing archive of over 100,000 negatives. The Ninomiya Photography Studio existed from the 1920's through the 1980's, most of that time in Little Tokyo, Los Angeles.

The staff at CSUDH's Gerth Archives; Special Collections Library is an amazing group of archivists and experts dedicated to the preservation of history and community. The Ninomiya Photography Archive is just a small and recent part of their huge collection.

My process was simple. I make an appointment. The staff selected boxes for my review. Each box was filled with sheets and sheets of images from a specific year and was often one of many boxes of that year. It took me about an hour to go through each box. Mostly, I studied the images and took photos of them if they interested me. I was drawn to photographs that were unique and/or exemplary of a trend I saw, either in regards to what the Ninomiya Studio was repeating in how they documented certain types of events or overall fashion trends that seemed so different to today's styles and cultural assumptions. In twelve months, I must have looked at around 3,000 photos.

Back at my studio, I looked at the shots I took and selected one or more from each session to translate into a small watercolor. Painting the watercolors forced me to engage with the photo image in a very detailed manner. Most of the photos were black and white, so I got to guess the color of the clothes, skin tone, eyes, lip stick, hair, etc.. Like drawing, your eye-mind-hand coordination is focusing on the minutiae of everything in that image. You begin to transport yourself back in time to what that moment might had been like. Looking at facial expressions or body language began to fill in the emotional content of that time and space. Narratives about relationships, attitudes and norms began to surface. Watercolor painting has a time element. The water will evaporate as it leaves the altered pigment in the crevices of the paper. The paint dries and bonds to the fibers in the paper and whatever happens is what you're left with. That transformation settles and you have to accept it. I always say that watercolors is the Raku of painting.

I had over twenty of these sessions in the Gerth Archive, often lasting three to five hours. These sessions had also afforded me to interact with staff. They exercised great patience with me. They are professional archivists. I am not. I suspect I approached the collection in a different way than they do, although there might be overlaps. We shared many mutual reactions to images and views on the historic significance and clues of certain images. Mostly, I feel like I learned from the staff. They have so many anecdotes that they shared with me, not only about what they've learned about the Ninomiya legacy but the nuts and bolts of what it was like to archive the collection. That was invaluable.

As part of my residency, I was asked to conduct four workshops; two with CSUDH students and two with art students from Banning High School. After the year in the archive, I had a solo exhibition in the university art gallery that was up for six months. My intention was to introduce the primary concepts of conservation to the students and my approach to the history using watercolors. I emphasized the importance of photography and how it played a role in history and related the importance of the family photo album.

One day, Gregory Williams, the Director of the Gerth Archive showed me some of the panoramas in the Ninomiya Photo Archives. These would have been taken by a special camera that would use a very long horizontal negative and were popular in the 1940's, 50's and 60's.

Why did the Ninomiya Photography Studio exist? Is it because white professional photographers wouldn't provide their services for Japanese and Japanese-Americans? On one hand, the Ninomiya's were allowed have a studio business but what does it say that, at least in the early years, the clientele was only Japanese. A decade after WWII, you begin to see the ethnic diversity of clients steadily transform. As you peruse the archive, you begin to see a vast horizon of time and the social norms that were exercised. In the 1960's and more so in the 1970's, you see more mix race weddings documented and non-Japanese portraits, the passport photos being a good example of this.

THE WRITTEN WORD

December 9, 2018

I need writers. My need to read began to grow in the fourth grade. I'm sure many people experienced this in school at around this period in their lives. It helped that one of my best memories of my late Father was seeing him reading in the living room or seeing a book on the table that I knew he was reading. These books were always in Japanese and often had a bookmark built into the binding. These bookmarks were thin ribbon like strands that would wear as the read would progress. He never made a big deal about it, he just read. We were not close. We didn't speak the same language and he was almost always at work. Our relationship was built through my Mother and observation. He worked really hard. He and I conversed maybe three times in my life and he did all the talking. I could sort of understand him but at the time I didn't have the skills to converse back to him. Reading was his intellectual solace and so it became mine's as well. We both needed writers.

I enjoyed learning. It was a way to get the inside scoop; like the backstage pass, like watching a rehearsal, reviewing the floor plan, unfolding the handwritten map. Books were access to things outside of my environment, although my environment was rich; Los Angeles' Koreatown. It cultivated the inner dialogue.

Reading took a quantum leap in Middle School or Junior High School as we used to call it. Alternative thoughts and new points of view through the written word were like stepping stones up a steep hill. I discovered new worlds: Mayan folktales, Shakespeare, Machiavelli and Rousseau. I was a fan of Thomas Jefferson's writings and always studied history through that democratic idyllic lens.

Is there anything more satisfying than the magic of the written word and how it affords the mind to build a world, a time and newness. The Watts Prophets said "Be New". Writing has often made me feel new; the pulse of a brand-new love or rediscovering how nature is not parallel to life but steering time.

I have never seen myself as a writer nor do I strive to become a writer. I have no hesitation or insecurity in expressing myself. I've been trained to express myself, actually. I am an artist but not a writer. I know writers. They are different. They create from a different part of the brain. They see the world differently. Their legacy is not my legacy. I have much respect for writers. I am attracted to writers. Certain works of writers have changed my life and influenced my art but I am not a *writer*.

When I go to a Writ Large Press event, my favorite literary community here in Los Angeles, even though I've been participating for years and was even featured once, I still feel like an outsider. I like being the other in this context and I suspect this segregation is partially self-imposed but absorbing their creativity and comradery, helps me get closer to understanding what it takes to master writing and in turn makes me a better reader. Reading is the action that my creative process benefits from and I'm convinced that the better I become at it, the stronger my art will be.

What I rely on is how writing offers discovery, through that other part of the brain, and then that discovered element helps me expand my art and then hopefully expands my audience. I've even titled works after books, passages or poems that inspired me. The creative muscle writers make possible for me is paramount and integral. They are doing the hard work that I get to benefit from. They access the place where they practice their voice and that inspires me as if it loosens the muscles around my muse.

Often, I am asked to write a description of my work, my mission statement or the thought process behind the making of my work. Early in my career, I would argue that if I could explain it in words, I'd be a writer. However, my perspective has changed. I understand now that writing about my work is not to define it but rather to create a bridge to the work. We demarcate the transaction of concepts with words. For instance, the exchange of words between two people are usually the arrowhead of social choreography but not the arrow. So, it makes sense that the writer has a powerful role in society. They are the mind's eye of community.

I met poet Nina Puro in 2015 at the MacDowell Arts Colony in Peterboro, New Hampshire, the U.S.'s oldest artist residency. The first time I met her, she had just arrived and was sitting on a bench outside the library. Nina had her laptop on her lap and when I walked out, she looked up and said hello. I hope I said hello back but there was already something about her that was spewing out of her presence that I could tell was unique. Several weeks later, we got to hear her recite her poetry and then I was hooked. Nina is able to form words and navigate the act of reading so that we can participate in what I would call the mysterious psycho-dance. I can explain it this way. Sometimes, for reasons I can't access, I fear the dark. I sense there's something there but I also know that this reflex is ancient and part of our survival mechanism. I venture forth into the dark anyway. That place between fear and fortitude; the rational and supernatural is where her work takes me; truthful and relentless. I told her once that, "Congratulations, you've captured the danger of solitude. It's (the poetry) devastating."

Chiwan Choi and I met through poet/writer Mike Sonksen and artist Nathan Ota, so naturally, part of my attraction to Chiwan is as a fellow Los Angeles Native and specifically Koreatown. I had met him and heard of him in reference to Writ Large Press, which he co-founded with Judeth Oden Choi and Peter Woods. It wasn't until I read his book of poems, *The Yellow House*, that it clicked. Here was a work that captured Koreatown in sensory illustrations that were exactly what I internalized. I had never seen anything so accurate, personal and thorough. *The Yellow House* is one of my most favorite works.

Mike Davis is a legend. Once described as a writer who wrote million dollar sentences, his opus on Los Angeles, *City of Quartz*, is still one of the most quoted books on anything under the topic L.A.. I first met Mike in 1996 when he co-taught at the Southern California School of Architecture with Adobe L.A.. Hearing him speak about a diverse array of topics from immigration to the old money of Los Angeles is like evaporating into time through anecdotes in a hailstorm of facts. I also enjoy hearing him talk about his life as a truck driver or his childhood. He exemplifies the idea that life is a continuum and non-linear, that is to say, ideology is a culmination not a dogma.

Eva Cockroft was a muralist, organizer and writer. I met her in 1990 when we both worked at the Social and Public Art Resource Center in Venice, CA. While I was there, she worked on her book, Signs From The Heart; California Chicano Murals. She was very encouraging about my art, which I was finding difficult to sustain while balancing a family and the job. I learned so much about what it took to publish a book, hearing her experiences almost daily. It was an amazing introduction to publishing but the broader implications were so much more important, i.e. that a visual artist could also write.

1973

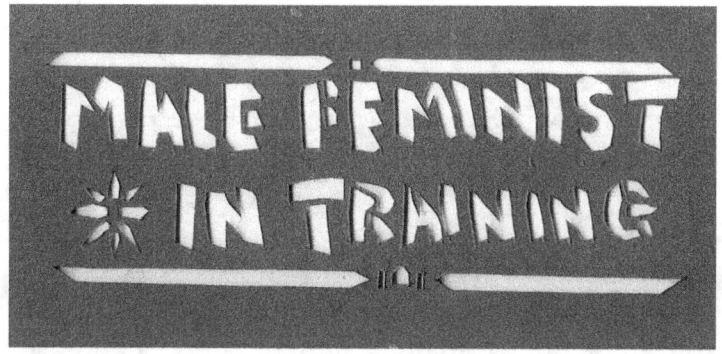

Was it in 1973? I would have been in the fourth grade at Wilton Place Elementary School. My elementary school teacher was Ms. Barbara Hokinson but that year she was diagnosed with cancer and Ms. Moy became our teacher early on. Ms. Hokinson survived cancer, in fact, when I returned years later as a college student at Otis Art Institute, she was teaching in the same classroom.

She didn't remember me but did remember my best friend Kenny and a few of the girls' names I was able to recall. Evidently, my life-long attraction to being allusive was early on. At that moment (an acne-ridden young adult with glasses) I was speaking with her (a very attractive older woman) as the alleged former student. It might have been my hormonal self, prone to fantasy, but she paid me a compliment that had innuendos. This has happened several times in my life where compliments are like salt to a garden snail. If only I were a little bit more savvy and quick, life might have been even more momentous but I guess that would be greedy.

1973; in the headlines were news like *the Battle of the Sexes*, a tennis match between Bobby Riggs and Billie Jean King (I was rooting for Billie Jean King); Gloria Steinem (I didn't understand exactly what she was talking about but I sensed she was right); Secretariat wins all the races (in a commercial decades later, we learn that this horse's heart is 3X the size of the average horse heart), the Cold War (our impending doom); Watergate (in the news a lot but I didn't understand what was going on exactly); Bruce Lee dies (the first movie I ever went to without my parents was *Enter the Dragon*. It played at the Wiltern Theater) and *Elvis Live in Hawaii* (amazing live footage, my Aunt was a big fan so I watched. My grandfather was born in Hawaii but moved to Hiroshima when he was nine).

My family was not political. They were your typical immigrant family from a WWII torn city trying to embrace the best Los Angeles had to offer but heavily insulated in a xenophobic bliss. I don't think anyone voted, for instance, and the only hint of politics I would hear about would be either at school or on TV. Certainly, there were no discussions about anything in the news or political at home.

Looking at Wikipedia under *1973*, I'm surprised to learn that in this year, the first Vietnam War POW's were released, Pablo Picasso dies, the World Trade

Center complex opens, Pink Floyd's *Dark Side of the Moon* is released, Skylab is launched, DJ Kool Herc originates Hip Hop (decades later I would co-produce the video *L.A. Hip Hop Volume One*), Pinochet overthrows the Chilean Government (later I would have the honor of working with Francisco Letelier) and the opening of both the films *The Sting* (I've never seen this film but enjoy the finger-nose sign-gesture they used and of course Scott Joplin's music was introduced to my generation through this film) and *The Exorcist* (to this day, I've never seen this film, too scared).

In 1973, I began taking lessons at the Shizue Yamashiro Art School near L.A. High School. The school was at Sensei's (teacher, jp.) second story apartment on Kenniston Avenue, where she lived with her husband, writer Mas Yamashiro.

You can say that I began my study of art and feminism in 1973, so to speak. This was a pivotal year for me. That same year, I was introduced to transcendental meditation and Antoni Gaudi's work. In retrospect, this may have been my most formative year; 1973.

Elementary or as it's known now Primary school is remarkable from the standpoint that potentially, you are with the same group of peers for five to six years of what are quantum leap years of growth, especially if you compare a kindergartener to a fifth or sixth grader as opposed to an eighth grader with a college undergraduate student, there's a ginormous dynamical change.

I do have a recurring memory of the sixth grade, my final year with such peer group. That is, we are out in a bustling playground during PE or Recess. In a moment of testosterone overload, perhaps watching too many martial arts movies, I said something to a female peer which made her upset. It was a rare and failed attempt to being the Alpha. She went off, evidentially to tell her entourage and all of sudden, I was encircled by the female guard of the sixth-grade class; angry, numerous, vociferous and enigmatic. I distinctly recall being unable to say anything in my defense, caught inexplicitly guilty. It was less a tribunal and more a riot. I remember thinking to myself, "this must be Feminism." Never did the playground bell sound so sweet. Sound, once again, saving my ass.

NALINI'S MELODY (LYRICS WRITTEN 2019)

Thank you for helping me across the street in Little Saigon
Your young smile and curiosity is what I love a ton
And yes, in the back of my mind, you remind me I was young
I wanted to say thank you for inspiring me to write a song

The artist that you want to be is stranded by some fears
You asked me about my process and how I oil my gears
Do by doing is what Ms. Rosenthal taught me in my early years
I say the greatest studio is the one between yours ears

From ancient times, Pre-internet, before the written word
The story was a song, a voice and something that you heard
Opportunity can fly away and time becomes an endangered bird
Just move forward is about the only way you can stay assured

I think your drawn to sewing leaves, cause it's like

sewing time
There are no dumb ideas, only limited minds
The greatest lessons down the road never were pre-
ceded by painted signs
Not carrying out your dreams is the ultimate crime
or a bad rhyme

Thank you for helping me across the street in Little
Saigon
Your young smile and curiosity is what I love a ton
And yes, in the back of my mind, you remind me I
was young
I wanted to say thank you for inspiring me to write
a song
I wanted to say thank you for inspiring me to write
a song

NEW YEARS RESOLUTION

Oral History; to discover things unsought through a conversation that is primarily one-sided

what is the psycho-geographical result of being lost in your hometown? or debunking the myth of the bohemian artist

the time and resource consuming apparatus of the romantic wandering mind

it's been fifteen plus years since my divorce. since then, I've been in a number of wonderfully educational relationships with exceptional people

i am going to turn 55 in three months

last night I was rejected. you know that feeling, don't you? the statement, let's be friends. it ends a week(s) , often month(s) long mental obstacle course of experiences together, misinterpretations and in this case , pure fantasy

is there a way to turn the system off?

as fabulous as sex is, as companionship is, as relational growth can be and the extinguishing of loneliness entices, I would like to and am trying to develop my artistic practice and portfolio for the remainder of my life antoni gaudi had his heart broken twice and ended up in a self-imposed monkhood living at the sagrada familia. his death was tragic but he focused on what became an incredible legacy in part paving the way for AutoCad.

to continue to go through life with this attraction to women and this wandering mind seems painful and a waste of time and resources

NEW YEARS RESOLUTIONS:
1) HEALTHIER GUT
2) NO PORK DURING THE YEAR OF THE PIG
3) PAUSE BEFORE STARTING ANY TYPE OF RELATIONSHIP. MANAGE YOUR BOUNDARIES. NOT EVERYONE NEEDS TO COME OVER FOR DINNER

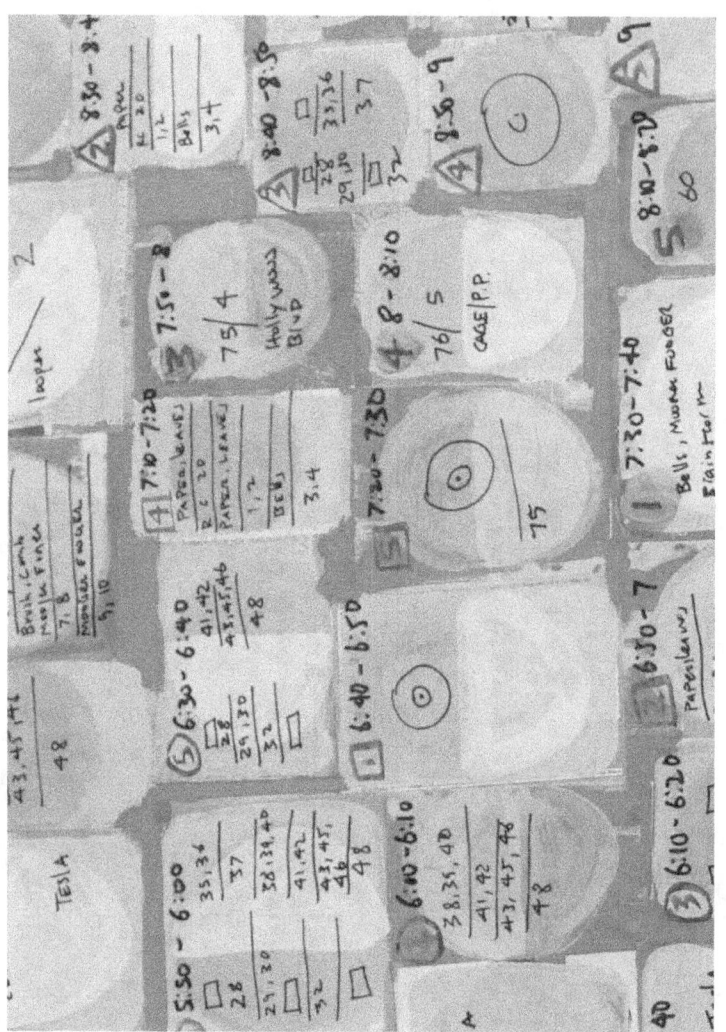

Organ of Corti Sound Map, ELA REP, 2013, image taken by Elon Schoenholz

WHEN I DIE

when i die
will it be the abyss?
non matter?
or is it hell for me?
you trained me to refuse the roles
so, so be it
there's nothing i can do to alter your predestined
nation
but if it's heaven
may i trade eternity
to help guide the one's i love?
not as an invisible human
but as a continual prayer
is that what you trained me to do?
i'd be up for that
it comes down to either a fire extinguisher or a
chemical transference
or are they in fact the same
is that what you're training me for?
i'd be up for that

PHOTOGRAPHY

(I wrote the following in response to my one-year research of the Ninomiya Photo Archive at California State University Dominguez Hills Library/Special Archives, where I was the A.I.R. through Praxis Arts from 2018-19, culminating in my solo show titled "Unfinished Proof Ninomiya" at the University Art Gallery, May 11 through September 18, 2019)

if time is a construct then we already have the ability to travel in it

the family photo album could be a vehicle

case study #1:
when I was very young, my grandfather pulled out his family photo album
as he thumbed through the pages he showed me young versions of him and my grandmother
i remember the experience as almost silent
all these various people, formally posed, black and white, in some cases sepia
to this day i have no idea who some of them were
i may never know but id like to
it's too late to ask him
i was actually scared of my grandfather so i probably never asked him anything
but there we were
a silent summer afternoon turning the pages of this old family photo album

and then it happened

i saw a tear in his eye
never saw him do that before or again
it freaked me out
no words
no actions
no response
no comprehension
just a little kid
an old man looking at a snapshot of his Mother

this is the privilege of being the first grandchild

if the cyberwars continue
and they will
the cloud is doomed
we will lose all of our images
our ability to time travel will be eliminated
the silos are already targeted

but

if we reestablish family photo albums
we would have a fighting chance for time travel

each home in possession of a portal
this would be nearly impossible to dismantle in a
cyberwar
a network of portals
memory would be intact

case study #2

in a survey, people were asked if their home was on fire, apart from family and pets, if they could take one item, what would that be? The overwhelming answer was their family photos

case study #3

in a study of holocaust survivors and their descendants
levels of cortisol were tested
this is the substance the body uses to combat stress
i.e. PTSD survivors have very low levels of cortisol
in the test of the holocaust descendants, cortisol levels were significantly low
suggesting that the stress of the holocaust continues through birth
even though the descendants had no direct experience

what is the difference between the body and the family photo album?

case study #4

in ancient times in japan
you were born into your family's craft
construction workers who used hammer and nails had a ritual
they believed that even though lumber was no longer a living tree
it still had the spirit of the tree inside

so, before each nail was hammered, they would apologize silently to the piece of wood

case study #5

when i worked for the social and public art resource center, coordinating murals across Los Angeles and later as a public arts officer for the la metro, i got to work with the late chieftess of the Gabriel/ Shoshone Nations, Vera Rocha.

i remember she told me that when the 105 Freeway was opened, she and her husband Manuel Rocha were asked to give a blessing. they asked that they conduct the ritual before the actual press event because they didn't want it to be photographed

unfortunately, a press photographer came early and took a photo of the blessing and published it in the newspaper that week. Vera Rocha was livid.

what was the violation?
what does this tell us about the power of the image?
what do we mean by sacred?

BEFORE I FORGET

(September 29, 2019, 4:50 AM)

I couldn't fall back to sleep again.
I've been lying awake analyzing a vivid dream.

In the dream, my Mom and Son were in a car driving through a LA neighborhood. My Mom is about twenty years younger and my Son is around six in this dream.

A flash of light in the daytime sky and an explosion nearby like a fallen craft and we found ourselves in front of it. It appeared to be a huge parachute or blimp crashed into a house like treehouse in the neighborhood. What's clear to me is that this aircraft must had been in the air and happened to be in the path of a crashing spacecraft.

The remnants of a crash, sort of like a steam punk crash scene in a sci-fi novel. Our car, as if in a tractor beam, elevated around the wreck which was three stories vertically. As we spun around, outside the three-story building we saw the strewn aircraft tangled into this odd building. At this point I realized we might see the remains of the victim of the crash so I covered my Mom's eye so she wouldn't see it. I think I said don't look to both my Mom and Son. Of course i did and so did my Son.

There was an older woman, large in stature, typing

away at a desk looking out into our eyes, a haunting encounter. She saw us. This was not human, it was a spirit. She was not happy to see us.

The next scene is we are now in the building and my son, who is an adult now in real life but in the dream is around six years old, and I are commenting on various items in the building. This tree-house-like-building is narrow with a wood spiral staircase, the quality of which is similar to the wood staircase at our house that leads from the second floor to the backyard. The interior was of a domestic, familiar, home.

I can't remember what the object was but it was like a folding tent you would bring to the beach, or something like that it flew up and grabbed us but we easily took it off. Was it haunted, did it mean harm or was it just having fun with us? We were trying to get out of there. There was no sign of that spirit we saw earlier.

That's when I woke up.

I lay in bed for a half hour analyzing the parts of the dream I can remember. Much of it clear, my spirit pounding. I think, as I often do at this hour, is this the result of sleep apnea? I had surgery for sleep apnea years ago but maybe it's come back?

I connected these dots which is why I wanted to document this dream and thought:
1) Seeing your life flash before your eyes (so often

mention in near death experiences)
2) Black hole
3) Collective unconscious

I had the sensation of thinking there is a tie between these three things, that in fact, that was symbolically what this dream was about.

The aftermath of a fatal event, perhaps not from this world or rather the collision between this world and another. The connection or bumping into of one world into another? A moment where parallels touch, an unreal explosion; extraordinary. The midair circling of the building and witnessing the remnants but also the physical entanglement. Was this death or fusion? Is fusion death or partially death? Part of fusion must be death, right? So, when two things join, even momentarily, it is explosive because it's new; new things sparkle. Most new things attract? Death attracts? Maybe the aftermath of death attracts? Like a funeral, where many meet or reconnect in honor of the dead. Funerals are no more for the dead than for the living. It's in honor of the deceased but it's also an affirmation of the living, of life. So, is a funeral social fusion?

What if the entirety of life flashing before your eyes was not only the moment of individual truth but also of glimpse into the collective unconscious? Maybe it's a flash moment? Maybe it's a passport, a threshold for a energy transfer? Maybe it's the end game, the final flash of our energy like a super nova?

Could there be a pool of all the lives flashing, spinning like eternal GIFs? The black hole could be a storage unit or mausoleum of every living things life flash, an eternal flash drive of memories; of every living thing of this world and all worlds in an infinity of galaxies multiplied by parallel universes.

Ok, I'm going to try to go back to sleep.

FEBRUARY 26, 2020

11:33 PM

I just got back from Drunken Masters. This is Writ Large Press' event that happens fairly regularly. A small roster of writers read a couple of poems and then three writers critique what was read as they keep drinking. Naturally, these always occur at a bar and tonight, it was at the General Lee's in the Chinatown Central Plaza. I so enjoy these. Much of the comments by the masters translate into ideas for my art. Actually, artist Ana Chaidez, was there tonight saying the same thing. As a visual artist, it helps to go to these literary events. It's a way to pick up ideas on how to approach your art in a different way.

I also enjoy the people who run this event, one of which is Chiwan Choi, who saw me and said he was ready to read my first draft of this book. Chiwan is a poet and is 1/3 of Writ Large Press, the publisher of this book. I realized, oh, this is the end of writing this book. That's right. That makes sense, this has to end at some point.

So one last thing I wanted to write about.

From March 2019 to now, I've been the A.I.R. for the Pasadena Buddhist Temple. It's been twelve months of amazing research and community building. A couple of months ago, as we were moving forward with the last project, it occurred to me that this community has embraced me being there in the most natural way. There had been much talk about my continuing a presence there as a member. Then, someone sent me an email from Creative Capital, a national art funder. Very quickly, we decided to write a grant for Phase Two of my A.I.R.

So, the projects continue after the end point of this book. If all goes as we would like it to go, my 12 months artist residency with the Temple will expand. If this happens, as you've read in this book, it'll be the first time I get to work in a community for more than one year. Suffice to say, all my experiences thus far have positioned me to be able to architect the continuation of such an opportunity. I would never have been able to position myself in this kind of position six or eight years ago. I hope this happens. The things I want to accomplish at the Pasadena Buddhist Temple will go far beyond anything I've ever done. Fingers crossed. I also want to say good luck to you too! I hope you find yourself in a similar position of opportunity and readiness.

A.I.R. AS A MUSCLE

as i keep working
i meet people
and what i am asked to do
is my job
this trajectory of labor
of our labor
of   my   labor
has been said to me, unique
but i suggest it's not so much
and maybe more specifically
it shouldn't be
this written work is my autobiography
but it's my attempt to make the complexities of being acknowledged apparent
because
when I show up
this is who you are meeting
and my work
is an attempt to acknowledge
your autobiography
the similar complexities in you
everyone
who shows up will dictate success
is a sum of their experiences?
yes, we wear the clothes of our heroes
but those clothes
those fashions and trends
those protections
like relics of our individual popular cultures
are our superhero capes
and only superheroes wear capes that fit

ALAN NAKAGAWA, ARTIST

CONTACT: invisibleteahouse @ gmail . com
WEBSITE: www.alannakagawa.com
Based in Los Angeles, CA USA

Alan Nakagawa is an interdisciplinary artist with archiving tendencies, primarily working with sound, often incorporating various media and working with communities.

Nakagawa has been working on semi-autobiographic sound-architecture/tactile sound experiences, utilizing multi-point audio field recordings of historic interiors; Peace Resonance; Hiroshima/Wendover combines recordings of the interiors of the Hiroshima Atomic Dome (Hiroshima, Japan) and Wendover Hangar (Utah); Conical Sound; Antoni Gaudi and Simon Rodia combines recordings of the interiors of Watts Towers (Los Angeles) and the Sagrada Familia (Barcelona, Spain).

He's in his fourth year as the artist-in-residence at the Pasadena Buddhist Temple through Side Street Projects, developing multi-disciplinary art projects in response to the history of the Temple and the Post-WWII Japanese American community it was founded by.

Nakagawa is also currently the artist-in-residence at the Gerth Archives, California State University Dominguez Hills assigned to the newly acquired L.A. Free Press/Art Kunkin Collection.

He was the first artist-in-residence for the Los Angeles Department of Transportation and the Los Angeles County Library. Nakagawa was invited by the Smithsonian Museum of American History to research the development of the hearing aid in the

US. He currently resides in Los Angeles' Koreatown and continues to exhibit and develop his creative practice.

Nakagawa is a recipient of two Art Matters grants, City of Los Angeles Artist Fellowship, California Community Foundation Mid-Career Artist Fellowship and a Monbusho Scholar. He co-founded arts collective non-profit Collage Ensemble Inc. (1984-2011), curated experimental music weekly Ear Meal Webcast (2010-2017) and produced public practice artist interviews podcast VISITINGS Radio Show (2017-2020).

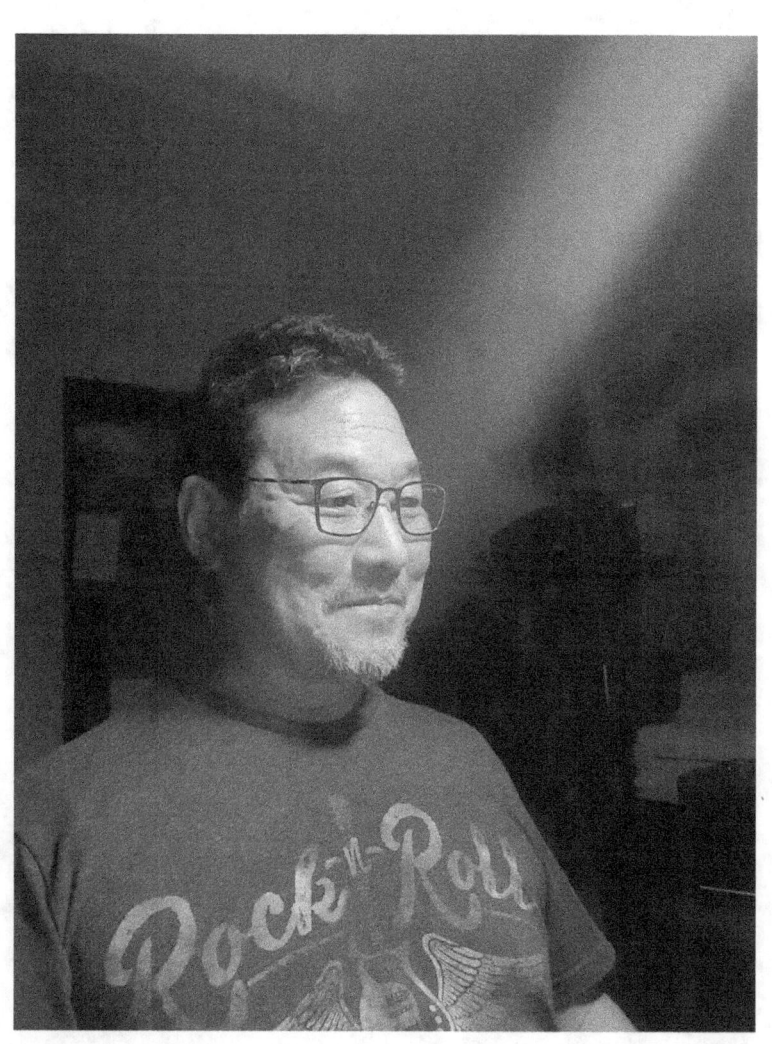